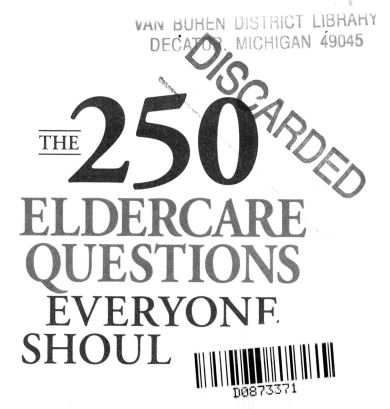

THE 250

ELDERCARE QUESTIONS EVERYONE SHOUL

LITA EPSTEIN, MBA

BUSINESS
Avon, Massachusetts

362.6
eps

Published by Adams Business, an imprint of Adams Media,
a division of F+W Media, Inc.
57 Littlefield Street, Avon, MA 02322. U.S.A.
www.adamsmedia.com

ISBN 10: 1-59869-890-7
ISBN 13: 978-1-59869-890-9

ı   Printed in Canada.

J   I   H   G   F   E   D   C   B   A

Library of Congress Cataloging-in-Publication Data
is available from the publisher.

This publication is designed to provide accurate and authoritative information
with regard to the subject matter covered. It is sold with the understanding
that the publisher is not engaged in rendering legal, accounting, or other professional advice. If legal advice or other expert assistance is required, the services of a competent professional person should be sought.
—From a *Declaration of Principles* jointly adopted by a Committee of the
American Bar Association and a Committee of Publishers and Associations

Many of the designations used by manufacturers and sellers to distinguish
their products are claimed as trademarks. Where those designations appear in
this book and Adams Media was aware of a trademark claim, the designations
have been printed with initial capital letters.

This book is available at quantity discounts for bulk purchases.
For information, call 1-800-289-0963.

CONTENTS

INTRODUCTION

Talking about financial and legal issues with our parents will be hard. Previous generations were taught to keep their financial and legal issues private. In addition, they may have difficulty accepting the reversal of roles when we become the decision-makers out of necessity.

Hopefully, your parents will never need you to be the decision-maker, but you can't count on that. Planning for the possibility that your parents or other family elders will become incapable of making financial and legal decisions will make it much less painful to deal with if the need arises.

There are many financial, medical, and legal documents that can be put in place while your elders are still able to make decisions that will ease the burden for all later. In this book, I'll introduce you to the key documents you should prepare and other things you should do to be sure that you are ready if the time comes when you must make the decisions for your parents or other family elders.

Chapter 1

GETTING STARTED— WHAT COMES FIRST?

PROBABLY THE HARDEST thing you'll need to do is start a conversation with your parents about their financial and legal situation. Most parents deliberately avoid discussing these topics with their kids. But now that your parents are getting older, this habit must change. In this chapter, I'll review the key things you must talk about and how to get the conversation started.

Question 1: **How do I start talking with my elderly parents?**

That depends upon your current relationship with your parents. If you are one of the lucky few who grew up in families in which legal and financial issues were discussed openly, this will be an easy conversation to start. If not, you're in the majority, and you'll likely find yourself dancing around the topic as you try to get your parents to open up about their financial situation and what provisions they've made for dealing with their finances as they age.

Your parents will most likely start by saying it's none of your business. Don't keep digging if that happens. Instead, start talking about your concerns and the issues you want to discuss. Begin talking generally about topics such as estate planning and making provisions for emergency medical situations. As you discuss the issues, your parents may open up and start talking about the plans they've already made. Or maybe they'll ask you for your help to get their plans in place.

If you do not succeed in getting your parents to open up, you may want to contact a local senior center and ask to speak with a counselor or social worker who helps families deal with these issues. Sometimes an uninvolved third party can help get the ball rolling more easily than you can.

Question 2: **What are the key topics I need to talk about?**

The key topics you need to talk about fall into three general areas:

- **Financial decision-making:** Discuss making provisions for handling your elder's finances should he or she become unable to do so. In Chapters 3 and 4, I'll cover the basics of what needs to be done to plan for incompetency and what needs to be done after your elder becomes incompetent. In Chapters 6 and 7, I'll discuss the basics of handling your elder's budget and managing his or her funds.

- **Medical decision-making:** If your elder is unable to make medical decisions for himself or herself, it's best if a family member has been designated as the authority to make those decisions. In Chapter 5, I'll discuss the legal documents you need to have in place so that someone can make medical decisions when necessary. In Chapter 8, I'll discuss dealing with the costs of your elder's medical care.

- **Estate planning:** Even if your elder doesn't have much money, it's a good idea to sit down with an estate planner. You'll ensure that everything is in place to minimize the need for probate and distribute the estate as your elder wants it distributed. Chapters 9 through 11 discuss the basics of wills and probates. Chapters 12, 13, and 14 deal with tax issues. Chapter 15 discusses gifts. Chapter 16 discusses trusts. If there is a family business involved, you'll need to discuss the transfer of that business, which I'll cover briefly in Chapter 17. Finally, you'll need to think about life insurance, which I'll cover in Chapter 18.

Question 3: **What are the key legal documents an elder should have in place?**

Even if you can't get your elder to discuss estate planning, you must be sure that your elder has several key legal documents in place:

- A will for the distribution of the estate. I'll talk about the importance of a will in Chapter 10.
- A living will that indicates medical choices should your elder be unable to make them. I explain the importance of living wills in Question 33.
- Designation of a medical decision-maker. I'll talk about various options in Chapter 5.
- A durable power of attorney or other legal document that specifies who will be in charge of your elder's affairs should he or she become incompetent (see Question 17).

Question 4: **What key financial planning steps should you take with an elder?**

Your first step should be to sit down with your elder and sort out his or her current financial position. You need to look at:

- Bank accounts
- Mortgages or other loans
- Credit card accounts
- Ownership documents (titles to houses, cars, or other assets)
- Life insurance policies

Once you've sorted all this out, you'll have a better picture of what you have to work with as you try to plan for the long-term care of your elder. If you believe that your elder's holdings are minimal and you feel confident that you can handle the financial planning for the rest of your elder's life, you can certainly make that choice, but I recommend that you sit down with a certified financial planner to get a second opinion. You don't have to do this regularly, but a one-time review of your elder's financial position will be a smart move. You need to be sure that he or she will have enough money to live on for the rest of his or her life. If not, you need to start figuring out what you can do to extend the life of your elder's finances. I'll talk more about budgeting in Chapter 6.

The financial planner also can be helpful as you and your elder make choices for the future. If you don't know a planner, the Financial Planning Association has an excellent tool that you can use to find a planner near you (*www.fpanet.org/plannersearch/search.cfm*).

Question 5: **Do I need help with estate planning?**

Probably. As you read the chapters on estate planning, you quickly will find that the information appears to be written in a foreign language. Yes, it's true: estate planning appears to have a language of its own, and if you don't prepare the documents in exactly the right way, the courts can determine that they are invalid and toss them out. The Internal Revenue Service (IRS) can determine that a trust was not set up properly, and you can end up having to pay a large portion of the funds left in taxes.

Don't make the mistake of thinking you can handle estate planning yourself. Sit down with an attorney who knows the laws of the state in which your elder resides, and make sure that the plans that are in place were made correctly according to that state's laws. Often, people have their estate documents prepared in one state and then move to another. Estate law is based on the laws of each state, and each state has its own set of rules.

Question 6: **What types of advisers should I seek out?**

As you sort out your elder's affairs, it's always good to get a third-party assessment of what you think you are seeing. You may experience a lot of emotion as you try to help your parents or other family elders, and you won't always be able to make an unbiased assessment of what needs to be done. Here are some types of advisers you may want to seek out:

- **Social worker or senior counselor:** If you are having trouble talking with your parents or other elders, don't start fighting and making things worse. Seek out a social worker or counselor who specializes in working with seniors to help you begin your discussions.
- **Financial planner:** As discussed in Question 4, your best bet is to have a certified financial planner review your elder's financial situation and help you put together a long-term plan. If your elder doesn't have enough money for the long term, you need to know that, too.
- **Estate planner:** As discussed in Question 5, estate planning is not for novices. You will need to seek out an attorney who is well-versed in the laws of the state where your elder resides to ensure that all of his estate documents have been prepared in accordance with that state's laws.

Question 7: **How do I find the right advisers?**

When you are looking for advisers, your best bet is always to ask for recommendations from the people you know and trust. If you can't find an adviser through friends and family, your next best stop is the professional association that certifies these professionals. For financial planners, the best stop is the Financial Planning Association (*www.fpanet.org*). For accountants, the American Institute of Certified Public Accountants (*www.aicpa.org*) should be your first stop. You also can check with the local bar association for a recommendation of an attorney who specializes in estate planning.

Chapter **2**

TAKING THE RIGHT STEPS TO COMMUNICATE

You MAY FIND it difficult to get your elder to talk about personal financial, medical, and legal issues. Don't push it. In this chapter, I'll review some basic techniques you can try. If none of them works, don't get into a fight. Instead, seek the help of a professional counselor or social worker who specializes in senior care.

Question 8: **How do I preserve an elder's autonomy but take the control I need to take?**

That's a tricky question, especially if your elder has always been the one in control and has never looked to his or her children for guidance. If your elder is reluctant to talk to you, make it clear that you respect his needs and concerns and that you don't want to make any decisions without his full involvement.

If you strike out on your first attempt, don't give up. Leave the door open to the possibility of bringing up the topic again, or suggest that your elder might feel more comfortable discussing the topic with a different family member. You may find that it's easier for him to talk with a sibling. Share your concerns with the sibling your elder suggests, and see if that sibling will help you open the door.

Once the door is open, always include your elder in any decisions you need to make. Even if your elder is not able to make those decisions, the fact that he is part of the decision-making process will help him to feel in control.

Question 9: **What types of communication work best to get an elder's attention?**

If your elder is resistant, it's best to start talking about issues that concern you. For example, you might start by talking about a medical emergency in which the person is unconscious and someone needs to make a medical decision for that person. If this happened earlier in life to you or another sibling, you can bring that up as an example. Then talk about how you are concerned about what would happen to your elder in this type of situation. Ask her if she has created a living will. Today, many doctors' offices and hospitals encourage people to complete a living will, so you may find out that your elder already has one in place. If she has created a living will, find out if she has named someone to make medical decisions if she cannot. As you get deeper into the discussion, you can bring up the need for a medical representative if one is not already in place.

By handling the discussion in this way, you involve your elder in a conversation about a problem that concerns you without telling her that she must do something. I can guarantee that your elder would balk if you started the conversation by asking her if she has appointed a medical representative; she would feel threatened. By taking the roundabout route, you get to where you want to go, but you do it gently. You fully involve your elder in the conversation and in doing some problem solving.

Question 10: **How can I avoid trying to take over and causing conflict?**

As I mentioned in my answer to Question 9, the key is not to discuss the issue head-on if you find that doing so causes conflict.

Instead, find a strategy for making a decision by discussing general issues that involve that decision.

Your elder will balk if you try to force him to make a decision that he is not ready to make. Take the time to discuss issues. If he keeps avoiding a particular issue, then move on to another topic and come back to it.

Make yourself a list of all the issues you need to discuss with your elder, and gradually work your way through that list each time you see him. If you meet resistance, don't push. Instead, try to come back to that issue at a later time. If an issue must be discussed because financial and medical decisions must be made, seek out a social worker or counselor who can help you get the issue resolved without conflict.

Question 11: **How can I make a deal with an elder to solve a problem in a way that satisfies both our interests?**

Dealmaking with your elder may be a bit more personal, but the techniques involved are no different from those you would use to make a deal in any real-life situation. Lay out all your concerns about what needs to be done. Make a list of how you and your elder can get those things done together. Then discuss each item, and determine who will do each of them.

If you can move the discussion away from emotions and toward an objective decision, it will be much easier to solve the problem. As with any deal, emotions can get in the way of finding a compromise. Talk through the emotions, and be sure that you understand what is behind them before you try to get to a final deal. Oftentimes, an unfounded fear drives emotions; if you can address that fear, you will find it easier to get to a solution.

Question 12: **When should I seek help in trying to communicate with an elder?**

Whenever you get to the point at which your elder shuts down and will not talk about something that needs to be talked about, you may want to seek help. You don't always need to seek out a professional. Sometimes another family member can help you get past a problem. But if the problem must be solved and no one in the family can get through to your elder, then you're better off seeking professional help than getting into a huge fight.

A professional will know how to ask just the right questions to find out what is truly blocking the needed decision. Often, a neutral third party can see communication problems that the two involved in the disagreement just can't recognize.

Question 13: **What type of help with communication might I seek?**

The type of help you might seek will depend on the issue. If the issue is medical, you may ask your elder if you can go with him to a doctor appointment to discuss the problem. If the issue is financial, you may suggest setting up a meeting with a financial adviser.

If the issue is just a situation in which the elder does not feel comfortable talking, then your best bet is to seek out a social worker or senior counselor. Usually, you can find a good senior counselor at a local senior center run by your elder's house of worship or by the local government.

Question 14: **How do I find the right type of adviser to help improve communication with an elder?**

You may be able to find an adviser within your family. A sibling or other family member who is close to your elder may be able to help you understand the barriers to communication and how to overcome them. If not, look for a social worker or senior counselor through your elder's house of worship or through a local senior center.

If none of these situations works for you, then talk with your elder's doctor, and see if he or she can recommend a good senior counselor in the area or at least a source for information. If all attempts to find someone to help locally fail, try calling the Eldercare Locator at 800-677-1116, or go to the website *www.eldercare.gov*.

Chapter 3

TALKING ABOUT AND PLANNING FOR INCOMPETENCY

ONE OF THE most difficult issues you will need to discuss with your elder is possible incompetency. Don't put off this conversation: waiting until the worst happens will prove much more difficult and expensive. At that point, you will need to involve the courts; I'll talk more about what that entails in Chapter 4. In this chapter, I will review the options you have to plan for possible incompetency.

Question 15: **How do I plan for the management of an elder's affairs should he or she become incompetent in the future?**

You will find incompetency difficult to talk about, but force yourself to have this conversation with your elder. That way, you will be able to take advantage of a number of options in planning for possible incapacity or incompetence. Without planning, you'll lose these options once the person becomes incompetent. Some cost nothing, others will involve minimal legal fees, and still others may involve the costs of setting up a trust. Choices include:

- Establishing a joint convenience checking account (see Question 16)
- Executing a durable power of attorney (see Question 17)
- Funding a revocable living trust (see Question 18)
- Funding a contingent revocable living trust in combination with a durable power of attorney (see Question 19)
- Setting up a special needs trust (see Question 20)
- Drafting a voluntary, limited conservatorship (see Question 21)

Question 16: **What is a joint convenience checking account?**

Opening a joint convenience checking account is the simplest thing you can do to set up a mechanism for handling your elder's finances. This type of account works best if the funds put into the account are needed for routine expenditures and if your elder needs assistance with routine bill paying.

Simply follow the rules required by your elder's bank to set up such an account. As long as your state laws authorize a joint convenience checking account, it's better to use this form of checking rather than an account with joint tenancy with right of survivor. With the convenience checking account, you will be limited as a cosigner to withdrawing funds solely for the benefit of your incompetent or incapacitated elder. Explain these limitations to your elder, and she will feel more comfortable with agreeing to a joint checking account.

If a cosigner on a joint convenience checking account uses funds for himself, there could be gift tax implications for the incompetent person. If there is any interest income on a joint convenience checking account, the income will be taxed.

Any money left in a joint convenience checking account after the incompetent person dies becomes part of the decedent's estate to be distributed based on the provisions in the will. Any money left in a joint tenancy account will go to the person who was the joint tenant and will bypass probate.

Question 17: **What is a durable power of attorney?**

A durable power of attorney creates an agency relationship between one person (who is the principal) and another person or institution (who is the attorney-in-fact). The scope of the durable power of attorney can be very broad, giving the attorney-in-fact permission to do any act the principal can do except to execute a will, or it can be very limited. For example, the attorney-in-fact can be given only the right to perform one specific act, such as to sell a piece of property.

When your elder is competent, he can set up a durable power of attorney as long as he has the legal capacity to appoint someone else to perform an act for him. State law determines who has the legal capacity.

Your elder can't use a traditional nondurable power of attorney for preplanning for incapacity because the powers of an attorney-in-fact cease when the principal is no longer legally competent to complete the act. In all fifty states, a durable power of attorney remains in effect even after the person is incompetent.

Question 18: **What is a funded revocable living trust?**

A revocable living trust is another option that can be used to prepare for the possibility of becoming incapacitated and unable to handle one's affairs. Usually the grantor of the trust (your elder) is also the trustee. To fund the trust, title all appropriate property by making the revocable living trust the holder of legal title to the property. In most cases, the grantor or the grantor and his or her spouse are sole lifetime beneficiaries of the trust. Your elder will continue to manage the assets of the trust, as well as his own finances, in the same way that he did in the past, but now as a trustee of the revocable living trust.

With all the legal work in place and the trust funded, the only action one needs to take when planning for possible incapacity is to draw up (or have drawn up) a trust document specifying what will happen if and when your elder becomes incompetent or dies. When your elder becomes incompetent, he will be removed as the trustee, and the full trust powers will go to a cotrustee or a successor trustee who was named while your elder still had the legal capacity to choose whom he wanted to manage the trust. The trust allows the assets in the trust to avoid probate and may also provide for the management of the property after your elder's death.

Since this will not be a completed gift because the trust is revocable, your elder doesn't have to worry about gift taxes. The total value of assets remaining in the trust when your elder dies will be included in the calculation of the gross estate for estate-tax purposes.

Question 19: **What is a contingent (standby) trust?**

If your elder doesn't want to fund a trust immediately, she might like the idea of a revocable living trust as the means to manage her property and finances if she becomes incapacitated. She can set up a contingent, or standby, trust with minimal funding (as little as $5) as long as you execute a durable power of attorney. The person named in this durable power of attorney as your attorney-in-fact will take responsibility for fully funding the trust and naming the trustee should your elder become incapacitated.

The power given to the person named in the durable power of attorney can be either immediate or "springing." Springing means that the durable power of attorney will not take effect until your elder becomes incapacitated. Your elder sets up the terms of the trust agreement and specifies the duties, powers, and discretion of the trustee, whom your elder can name.

Should your elder become incapacitated, the attorney-in-fact changes the title of the principal's assets from the principal to the trustee. The trustee then manages the property based on the terms set when the trust was set up.

Question 20: **What is a special needs/Craven trust?**

A special needs, or Craven, trust is an irrevocable trust set up for the benefit of someone else. Often this type of trust is set up by a parent for the care of a disabled child or by an adult child for the care of an elderly parent. The trustee usually is given discretionary power over the distribution of the income from the trust.

If the trust is created during the grantor's life, the trust income will be taxable either to the trust or to the income beneficiary because the trust is irrevocable.

If the grantor retains too much control over the trust distributions or if the trust distributions are used to pay a legal support obligation, then the trust income will be taxable to the grantor.

If the grantor relinquishes all control in the trust, the assets of the trust will not be included in his gross estate. But if the grantor retains too much control, the assets will be included in his gross estate. Creating and funding the trust during the grantor's lifetime could result in gift taxes.

Question 21: **What is voluntary, limited conservatorship?**

Another option for managing your elder's financial affairs is a voluntary, limited conservatorship. Not all states authorize these types of conservatorships, but if your state does, your elder has the right to pick the conservator and control his or her powers. Your elder also can more easily dissolve a voluntary, limited conservatorship than he can if the state mandates a conservatorship.

This type of conservatorship is based on the fact that the conservator will need to deal with only part of one's financial affairs. For example, this type of conservatorship might be used if your elder can continue to handle routine, smaller expenditures but needs help with large sums of money or major purchases.

The primary advantages of this type of conservatorship are that your elder gets to pick the person who will handle his finances, and avoids the stigma of being found to be totally incompetent. Your elder still will need to go before the court to establish the conservatorship.

Chapter 4

PROBLEMS OF INCOMPETENCY

SO WHAT HAPPENS if you're not able to talk about incompetency planning with your elder? You will need to face the courts. In this chapter, I'll review what happens when you don't plan for incompetency.

Question 22: **Who can be considered incompetent?**

People of any age can lose their ability to manage the basics of daily life and care for their property or financial affairs. A person can be considered incompetent if he lacks the ability to communicate responsible decisions concerning his personal life or financial affairs.

A minor child who has not reached the legal age of majority in the state in which she lives—which is twenty-one in most states and eighteen in other states—is considered incompetent. An adult with diminished capacity also can be considered incompetent. Mental illness or deficiency, physical illness or disability, advanced age, chronic use of alcohol or drugs, confinement, detention by a foreign power, or disappearance can result in incompetency.

Question 23: **Why don't people plan for incompetency?**

Most people don't expect to be incapacitated and have no idea what problems incompetency can cause. They think that they will be in good health until it's their time to die. Others who may be aware of the possibility don't want to think about such an unpleasant situation. Probably the most common reason is procrastination.

Sometimes people understand the need to plan for the possibility of incompetency but decide that they just don't like any of the planning techniques or don't want to pay any of the up-front costs, such as fees to a planner or attorney to execute the necessary documents. Others may decide not to plan because they don't want to hurt the feelings of a family member or friend by choosing someone else to manage their affairs.

Question 24: **What are state-mandated court-ordered arrangements for people to handle the financial affairs of an incompetent person?**

If your elder doesn't plan for incompetency, the state mandates a court-ordered arrangement. So exactly how your elder's financial affairs will be handled if your elder becomes incompetent will depend upon the laws of the state in which your elder lives. The state will appoint a guardian to take responsibility for both your elder and her property when she is declared incompetent (see Question 25 about guardianship).

Question 25: **What is guardianship, and how does it work?**

Guardianship involves any arrangement in which a person takes responsibility for the care of another person and his or her property. Court-ordered guardianship will provide for the care of an incompetent person. The guardian or guardians of an estate, when ordered by the court, will manage an incompetent person's financial affairs.

Plenary guardianship is a court-ordered arrangement that involves the complete control of an incompetent person and her property. It includes the person's daily activities, living arrangements, nonemergency health care, and any other necessary activities. In addition, it includes the management of the incompetent person's financial affairs, which results in the loss of her basic civil and property rights.

The person who is deemed incompetent becomes a ward of the state. The court-appointed guardian acts under and within the state's authority to protect the ward in a fiduciary capacity. Most states have a list of priorities for appointment of a guardian based on the relationship to the adult incompetent person. First will be a person who held the most recent durable power of attorney. Next will be a spouse or person designated in the incompetent person's will. Next will be an adult child, followed by any family member with whom the incapacitated person has lived in the past six months. The last choice will be a person nominated by the person who is caring for or paying for an incapacitated person's care.

Question 26: **What is conservatorship, and how does it work?**

A conservator is a court-appointed person who protects and manages the financial affairs of an incompetent person. A conservator can be appointed if the court finds that a person needs protection because she is unable to manage her property. In addition, the court must find that the property owned by the incompetent person might be wasted unless proper management is provided. A conservatorship also can be mandated if the court finds it is necessary or desirable to protect assets so that there will be funds available for the person's support, care, and welfare.

Question 27: **How do I establish a guardianship or conservatorship?**

Any person who has an interest in a person's welfare can file an action with the court. In many cases, the person who files a court action will be a family member. Because a court mandate could result in the person's loss of civil and property rights if he is declared incompetent, the person will be represented by a guardian ad litem (a person appointed by the court to protect his rights during the court proceedings). Lay and expert testimony regarding why the person should be declared incompetent will be presented to the court. If the court agrees with the person filing the action, it will appoint a guardian or conservator and will declare the person incompetent.

Question 28: **What are the powers and limits of guardianship and conservatorship?**

The state mandates specific powers to a guardian or conservator. The powers and limits to those powers include the following:

- A guardian for a minor has the powers and responsibilities similar to those of a parent. He will be responsible for the minor's support, care, and education but is not personally liable for the minor's expenses or liable for acts done by others on behalf of the minor.
- A guardian for an incapacitated person has any powers that are necessary or desirable to provide continuing care and supervision.
- A conservator has the powers necessary to manage and distribute the incompetent person's property for her support, education, care, or other benefits the conservator deems desirable. The only power a conservator does not have over an incompetent person's finances is the power to make a will.

Question 29: **What are limited guardianships?**

Every power and duty given to a guardian deprives the incapacitated person of civil and property rights, which can include the right to control his living arrangements and daily activities. A limited guardianship imposes restrictions on the guardian's powers, allowing the person who has been declared incompetent to make some decisions himself. A limited guardianship encourages the maximum self-reliance and independence of the incapacitated person.

Question 30: **What are limited conservatorships?**

Like a guardianship, a conservatorship deprives the incompetent person of civil and property rights, which may include the right to write checks, the right to make gifts, the right to contract with others, the right to buy and sell property, and the right to sue and be sued. A limited conservatorship restricts the powers of the conservator to handling specific transactions or types of transactions as manager of specific areas of the incompetent person's financial affairs.

Question 31: **What are the advantages of guardianships and conservatorships?**

The primary advantage of a guardianship is that it provides for continuing care and supervision of a minor's or incapacitated person's living arrangements and daily activities. The advantage of a conservatorship is that it protects and productively manages an incompetent person's property and other financial affairs. Another advantage is that the court has supervisory and enforcement powers to ensure that a guardian or conservator is acting in a fiduciary capacity to protect the incompetent person according to the state's authority.

Question 32: **What are the disadvantages of guardianships and conservatorships?**

Although you or your elder might like the idea of letting the courts make the tough decisions about incompetency so that neither of you has to plan for it, consider the disadvantages of court-ordered arrangements:

- They can be dehumanizing, since most states require that a person be declared mentally ill or incompetent before they will step in. Evidence must be presented to the court.
- They can be uncertain, time-consuming, and costly. Papers must be filed, expert testimony must be arranged and paid for, and if anyone challenges the incompetency, both sides must be represented in court.
- They can be inflexible in the powers granted. In most situations, the arrangements are not tailored to the specific situation.
- They may be uncertain regarding who will care for the person or manage the person's property. The person appointed may not be the one desired by the incapacitated person.

Chapter **5**

LEGAL DOCUMENTS YOU NEED TO HANDLE YOUR ELDER'S MEDICAL NEEDS

MAKING MEDICAL TREATMENT decisions when your elder needs care but is unable to make his own treatment decisions can be very difficult. You may not know exactly what type of care your elder would want in certain medical emergencies. The best way to avoid this uncertainty and to be sure that you are requesting the medical care your elder wants is to set up a living will. In this chapter, I will review the key documents you should have in place before you need to make a medical decision for your elder.

Question 33: **What are living wills?**

If you want to be certain that your elder's wishes about medical treatment are followed even if he becomes incompetent, make sure that he puts those wishes in writing, using a living will. This document will state your elder's intentions and give specific directions concerning medical treatment in the event that your elder becomes terminally ill or injured and is incapable of granting or withholding consent for treatment.

The most common purpose of a living will is to state one's wishes to be allowed to die without the application of life-prolonging measures one believes are futile. The living will also can be used to request certain types of treatment or pain relief, including artificial respiration or ventilation, heart pumping, dialysis, certain types of pain medications, and artificial feeding. The best type of living will specifies when one wants these procedures done and when one wants them withheld.

For example, your elder may want these procedures withheld if he is in a coma and if he is not expected to wake up. States set the rules for when these provisions are honored and when they can be ignored. Some states consider the living will to be a guide to medical providers. Ultimately, the medical provider is the one who decides if the patient's condition is terminal, or meets other specified wishes of the patient in accordance with the living will. If your elder does make a living will, be sure that he discusses the provisions that are important to him with his medical provider.

Question 34: **What is informed consent?**

Each time a person needs medical treatment, she or someone else must give consent for that treatment. This type of consent is called informed consent. The U.S. Supreme Court has ruled that a person who is recognized as competent has the right to refuse unwanted medical treatment.

Each state has the right to set up appropriate procedures for informed consent. Some states recognize the right to refuse life-sustaining treatment, and others permit the right to withhold or withdraw treatment. Even if family members and a patient's physician disagree with a patient's choice to withhold or withdraw treatment, the patient's right to decide is key as long as the patient is considered capable of understanding the consequences of her decision.

Question 35: **What is substituted judgment?**

Sometimes a patient is no longer capable of making decisions or communicating those decisions to her doctor, so she cannot give her informed consent to proposed medical treatments. When this happens, a family member, a friend, or someone else in the health care system will need to make all medical decisions for the incompetent person. This type of situation can be handled in two ways:

1. If the patient's wishes are known and were conveyed to a family member or friend, the court usually will respect the wishes of the incompetent person even if the wishes are not in writing.
2. If the patient's wishes are not known, the court uses the doctrine of substituted judgment. Under this rule, family members or others close to the person are authorized by the court to make medical decisions for the incapacitated patient because the courts have ruled that these people will know the patient's feelings and value system best.

If your elder doesn't plan for incapacity, she will have no control over who can make medical decisions for her, and her wishes will not be in writing. If your elder has specific feelings about when and if life-sustaining treatment should be withheld or withdrawn, make sure that she puts them in writing while she is still able to do so.

Question 36: **Why designate another person to make medical decisions?**

In most states, the living-will law applies only if an incompetent person's condition is terminal, so your elder still should designate another person to make medical decisions for her if she becomes incompetent but is not considered terminal. The person your elder designates also can make sure that her medical provider follows her wishes as specified in the living will. The person your elder designates can use his or her authority to either litigate to enforce your elder's wishes as stated in your elder's living will or to change medical providers. The designated person will be able to make decisions on issues that are not covered in your elder's living will because the court will deem that person knowledgeable of your elder's wishes and values, as well as of any specific instructions your elder may have given to her appointed agent.

Your elder can appoint someone to make medical decisions for her if she becomes incompetent by completing a health care proxy (see Question 37), by appointing a health care agent under specialized state statutes (see Question 39), or by appointing an attorney-in-fact using a durable power of attorney for the purpose of making medical decisions (see Question 17).

Question 37: **What is a proxy appointment?**

In some states, your elder can designate someone by proxy appointment to make medical decisions for her if she should become incompetent. A proxy appointment can be included in your elder's living will. Other states require one to make a proxy appointment in a separate document. Proxies can act only when the person who made the designation is in a condition specified in state statutes, which is usually when the person is in a terminal condition as defined in the statute.

Question 38: **What is a medical power of attorney?**

Another way to provide for a health care agent is to use a separate document called a durable power of attorney for health care or a document that meets the medical treatment decisions statute of your state. These types of documents allow a person to make health care decisions for your elder, including a decision to withhold or withdraw life support.

Your elder also can appoint an attorney-in-fact using a durable power of attorney (see Question 17). Although this type of document is usually used in conjunction with the management of money or property, there is nothing in state statutes or court decisions that restricts the durable power of attorney in such matters. Some states require the use of a durable power of attorney for health care, so be sure to seek legal advice in your state.

 A health care agent or a medical attorney-in-fact appointed under the durable power of attorney can usually make decisions for an incapacitated person whether or not the incapacitated person is terminal. The powers granted to an attorney-in-fact for health care decisions can be broad or limited. There are variations in each state regarding the amount of power that can be granted.

Question 39: **What is a medical-decision-making agent?**

A medical-decision-making agent is anyone designated to make medical decisions for a person using a medical power of attorney. In most states, a medical-decision-making agent also can be a medical attorney-in-fact who was appointed using a durable power of attorney. Some states will accept one's medical-decision-making agent only if a durable power of attorney for health care is in place.

In whatever document your elder decides to use to appoint her medical-decision-making agent, be sure that she specifically gives that person the appropriate authority:

- To have access to her medical records and the ability to disclose those records to communicate her previous treatment decisions
- To have the power to interpret her living will
- To have the power to give, refuse, or withdraw consent for specific medical or surgical measures based on her condition, prognosis, and known wishes
- To employ, discharge, and grant releases to medical personnel
- To start legal action, if necessary, and to get authorization for specific treatment decisions

- To spend or withhold funds needed to carry out medical treatment

Question 40: **What are medical directives?**

A medical directive is any directive written in advance of becoming ill and pertains to treatment preferences. The medical directive also will designate a person who can make decisions for your elder in the event that your elder becomes unable to make those decisions on her own behalf. The three most common types of medical directives are living wills, powers of attorney, and health care proxies.

Question 41: **What is a do-not-resuscitate order?**

A do-not-resuscitate order (DNR) is an order specifying that if the signatory's heart stops or if she stops breathing, no one should attempt to resuscitate her. As long as the patient is competent, she can sign this order and specify that it is in effect until she revokes it. Hospital procedures are in place to determine how to make DNR decisions, resolve disputes that may arise among medical personnel or family members, and protect the patient's right to refuse treatment in such emergency situations.

If a patient is incompetent and has no DNR in place, then the decision is usually made after the medical providers have consulted with family members, friends, a legal guardian, or a court-appointed representative. A living will can play a crucial role in this decision if the patient refuses artificial life-sustaining procedures in that will under certain circumstances.

Chapter 6

ASSESSING YOUR ELDER'S INCOME AND BUDGET

GETTING DOWN TO the nitty-gritty on budget may be a difficult bridge to cross, especially if your family has always avoided discussing finances. If both your parents are still around, this will be very difficult. You will have an easier time if the parent who always managed the finances has already died and the parent who is left knows little about his or her financial situation. In this chapter, I'll review the basics of budgeting, but you may find this topic too difficult to touch until you've opened a strong line of communication and trust. Don't fight about this topic, unless it becomes necessary for you to take over.

Question 42: **How do I determine how much income an elder has, and where it comes from?**

Your elder probably has several sources of income. Here's a list of sources to check:

- Many seniors have a traditional pension and get a monthly check. Although these types of pensions are disappearing, if your elder or his spouse worked for a major company, look for a pension payment.

- Most seniors get checks from Social Security. These checks come once a month and often are directly deposited into a checking account designated by the recipient.
- There are many possible sources of income from investments. These can include retirement and nonretirement savings. Track down income from these sources by looking at statements from the brokerage houses, banks, or mutual funds that hold the accounts.
- Many seniors work part time to supplement their income, so your elder may be getting a paycheck.

After you've sorted out all the possible sources, try to come up with a monthly income estimate. You will find this difficult if a significant amount of the income comes from investment sources, because that income could vary each month. If this is the case, you may need to look at year-end statements from the previous year and develop a monthly estimate of those funds.

Question 43: **How do I determine how much savings an elder has?**

Your elder likely has a number of different sources for savings, which may include the following:

- Retirement accounts—These can include a traditional independent retirement account (IRA), a Roth IRA, a 401(k) with your elder's former employer (less likely today, as most companies encourage people to transfer funds to IRAs), a cash-balance plan with a former employer, and other employer-based savings.
- Traditional savings accounts
- Bonds—Many people feel safest investing in government bonds, so be sure to ask about those. You may find that your elder has a drawer full of bonds or bonds stored in his safe-deposit box.

■ Nonretirement investment accounts

Try to find year-end statements that were used to calculate taxes. Typically, you'll find statements for multiple accounts stored in the same place.

Question 44: **How do I determine what kind of debt an elder has?**

Hopefully you won't find much, but as the costs of medications, food, utilities, and transportation continue to soar, more and more seniors find that they must depend on credit cards just to get by. Their fixed income continues to go down as costs continue to rise.

You may find that your elder doesn't even know how much debt he has. Your best bet is to review his checkbook to see what bills he pays. Also, check his mail for a month so that you can be sure that you've located all the debt your elder has.

Another source of debt could be doctors and hospitals. Medicare doesn't cover medical costs completely, so you may find that your elder has medical bills that need to be paid.

Your elder also could still have a mortgage. Don't forget to look for signs that he's still paying off his home. Once you have all the pieces put together, make a list of all outstanding debt.

Question 45: **Who should pay off an elder's debt?**

If your elder has a lot of debt, you'll need to make some difficult choices. You could determine that there is no way for your elder to ever pay off that debt. If you decide that you can't help, you may want to consider filing for bankruptcy to clear out the debt. Your elder likely won't be looking for new loans, and this could be a way to ease the monthly costs.

Remember that if you do make the choice to file for bankruptcy for your elder, you likely will need to assist with future credit applications. Most states do allow a person who has filed for bankruptcy to hold onto his home, provided that the person can pay the mortgage. Be sure that your elder will be able to either stay in his home or live elsewhere.

Question 46: How do I determine if an elder has enough money to pay for food, housing, and medication?

After you get a full assessment of your elder's income, savings, and debt, you need to determine whether or not your elder has enough money to pay for food, housing, and medication, as well as any other medical costs. If you determine that your elder is running short month after month, you'll then need to decide whether you and your siblings can help to support your elder in his current living situation or whether you'll need to move your elder to one of your homes or to another more affordable living situation.

Suppose your elder has decided to stay in the family home, which is much larger than your elder needs. You may decide that it's time to encourage your elder to sell the home and move into something he can more easily afford. Even if the house is paid off, if there is enough equity in the home, the extra cash could make it easier for your elder to pay the bills.

Another option your elder may want to consider is to take a reverse mortgage. I'll talk more about the pros and cons of a reverse mortgage in questions 60 and 61.

Question 47: How do I determine if an elder's retirement accounts are being withdrawn at the proper rate?

If your elder has funds in traditional IRAs or employer-funded retirement plans, such as 401(k)s or 403(b)s, he will have to follow the rules for distribution set by the IRS. One your elder reaches 70 ½, he must start withdrawing money from those plans.

You can find the rules for withdrawing these funds in IRS Publication 590 (*www.irs.gov/publications/p590/index.html*). Check these rules out carefully because the penalties for errors can be high. I'll discuss the penalties involved in my answer to Question 48.

Question 48: **Can an elder face penalties if enough money is not withdrawn from retirement funds?**

If your elder doesn't withdraw enough money from his retirement accounts, the penalties can be very high. If your elder doesn't take out the minimum amount required, he will have to pay a 50 percent penalty on any shortfall. If your elder took out $1,000 less than he was supposed to take out of his retirement savings account, then the penalty he would have to pay would be $500. It's much better for your elder to have that money in his pocket rather than to have to give it to the IRS, so be sure that your elder is carefully calculating distributions each year based on the IRS rules in Publication 590 (*www.irs.gov/publications/p590/index.html*).

Question 49: **How do I determine if an elder has appropriate insurance coverage, and if can it be restructured to reduce expenses?**

When looking at insurance, you should review property and casualty insurance, medical insurance, and life insurance. I'll talk about life insurance options in greater detail in Chapter 18, so I won't review the issues here.

Many elders drop property and casualty insurance as bills get tight. This can be a big mistake; a fire or natural disaster could result in a large loss that your elder could never pay. Review current property and casualty policies to make sure that your elder has the proper coverage. Also check the amount of insurance on the property. If an insurance company doesn't automatically update the amount covered, the value of the home as stated in the policy may be considerably lower than the actual market value.

It's wise to include a rider that updates the house to current code. If repairs are needed and the original work on the house is not up to code, your elder could end up spending a lot more money. If you don't have the code rider, the insurance company can subtract a sizeable portion of the bill, saying that portion was paid to bring the house up to code.

I'll discuss medical coverage in greater detail in Chapter 8, so I won't discuss that type of insurance here.

Question 50: **What kind of senior services might be available to help?**

Many communities offer a variety of senior services that make it easier for elders to live on their own. These include transportation services, day care services, and senior centers.

Call the department responsible for senior services in the county in which your elder resides, and ask to talk with a coordinator. Ask about the services offered, and find out the costs for using these services. Once you know what's available, you can then talk with your elder about the options. Can any of the available services help your elder minimize costs? Anything you can do to make it easier and more affordable for your elder to continue to live on her own will be greatly appreciated and will help you to build a more trusting relationship when you try to deal with the more difficult issues involving finances, medical care, and estate planning.

Question 51: **Who should pay for housekeeping?**

You may find that your elder, who has always done the housekeeping herself, now needs help. This can become an emergency if you go to your elder's home and find that she obviously hasn't cleaned for a while. The odors might make it apparent that this is a task your elder can no longer do.

Ask neighbors if they can recommend a cleaning person, and discuss the option with your elder. If she is interested, go ahead and arrange for the cleaning. If you find that your elder hasn't arranged for housekeeping because she can't afford it, you'll need to work with her to develop a budget that covers the cost. You may find that your elder does not have the money, and you'll have to ask other family members if they can chip in. This situation also could lead to a discussion about whether the home is now too big for your elder to take care of; maybe she should consider moving into something smaller that would be easier for her to take care of herself.

Question 52: **Who should pay for interior and exterior maintenance of an elder's home?**

Another common item that gets put off as our elders' finances get tighter and tighter is home maintenance. If your elder lives in a community with a homeowner's association that mandates a certain level of exterior maintenance, this can become a legal issue. When maintenance is not completed as required by a homeowner's association, the association can impose fines, which it can place as liens on a home.

As with housekeeping, if you find that this is no longer something your elder can afford to do, you will need to find out if your siblings can help with the costs. Some counties have programs for seniors that help with outside maintenance and repair for free or for a nominal cost. Find out if the county in which your elder lives offers such a program. You also may find that the church or synagogue your elder belongs to offers help to seniors.

Question 53: **Who should pay for home and appliance repairs?**

When you get to your elder's home, you may find that appliances are going unused because they don't work anymore. If your elder has any type of extended warranty on these items, make arrangements for a service person to come in. If not, just as with housekeeping and maintenance, you will have to figure out how to pay for repairs if your elder doesn't have the money. As you find that there are more and more things that need to get done but aren't getting done because of lack of funds, you are building your case for convincing your elder to consider a smaller, newer living arrangement—unless, of course, you have the money and can supplement her income.

Question 54: **Who should pay for any necessary remodeling satisfy an elder's living needs?**

You may find that your elder's home needs extensive remodeling in order for her to continue living there. This usually becomes an issue if an elder can no longer handle stairs or must use a walker or wheelchair. Also, if your elder becomes prone to falling, you may find that you need to put in handicap rails in the bathroom and along certain hallways.

Again, this can be a significant cost, and you must determine who will pay for it. If you have the funds to pay for remodeling yourself, or if you can put together the funds with other family members, this can be the easiest solution. If you can't afford to remodel your elder's home and neither can she, you may face an emergency situation. You will have to determine if there is a safe way for your elder to stay in her home. A fall can lead to a major medical problem.

If your elder is in a wheelchair, you may find that doorways are no longer big enough to accommodate it. Expanding doorways throughout the house can be a very expensive fix. Often, buying or renting a home designed for handicapped access makes much more sense then renovating an older home. Consider all options before deciding to do major renovations on an older home. Such a situation could help to build the case to encourage your elder to move into a new, smaller home that she can more easily afford.

Question 55: **Who should pay for assisted-living services?**

Your elder might require so much assistance that she needs to hire a home health aide or move into an assisted-living facility. If your elder needs help at home, and it is ordered by a medical doctor, Medicare may pay for part of the cost. I'll talk more about what Medicare pays for in Chapter 8.

If your elder has long-term-care insurance, you will be able to tap that policy, provided that a doctor orders the assistance.

Hopefully, your elder already has the insurance in place. If not, you won't be able to get it once your elder becomes ill.

Generally, you can get the best price for long-term-care insurance if you buy it between the ages of 55 and 60. You should always buy a policy with a guaranteed monthly premium for life. Such policies are more expensive on a monthly basis at first, but you'll still be able to afford them later in life when you actually need the care.

If your elder doesn't have long-term-care insurance and has used up whatever Medicare will pay, you again are in the situation of who can help pay for the care. Often families in this situation end up moving their elders into the homes of relatives who can provide the needed assistance. This may be your only option if you have no way to pay for assisted-living services.

Question 56: **Who should pay for alert systems?**

As your elder gets older and is living alone, the chances that she will take a fall or need emergency medical services increase. If your elder falls or experiences a heart attack or stroke, she may not be able to get to a telephone. There are services available that ensure that your elder will get emergency help. Your elder can wear a small device with a button that she can push to call for help. You and your elder may decide that this is the best thing to do if she wants to continue living alone. Medical Alert, LifeStation, and Lifeline are the three most popular systems available on the market today. As with all other budget items, you will need to figure out how to pay for the system. These systems usually cost about $30 per month.

Question 57: **Who should pay for an elder's travel expenses?**

While your elder is still able to travel, you should factor travel expenses into his budget. You'll need to decide who will pay for travel. In many families, the siblings share the costs by paying for travel to their homes or when they include their elder on a trip. Unless your elder has a sizeable monthly income, travel is probably something for which there will not be room in the budget.

Question 58: **How do I plan for emergency travel needs?**

If your elder needs to travel for emergency purposes and you don't have any room in the budget to set aside an emergency account, you will need to fund the trip or ask your siblings for help. If no money is available, you may need to draw additional funds out of the retirement savings accounts that particular month.

Question 59: **Should an elder consider raising additional cash using a reverse mortgage?**

If your elder has a lot of equity in her home and she is planning to stay there, a reverse mortgage may be a good option. These mortgages can be structured to allow your elder to stay in her home for life while receiving a set monthly amount rather than paying back the bank.

If you decide to consider this option for your elder, make sure that you involve an attorney who understands how to structure reverse-mortgage contracts. You will find some crooks out there who just want your elder's home and will not worry about her needs.

There are three types of reverse mortgages:

1. **Single-purpose reverse mortgages**, offered by some state and local government agencies, are for a specific purpose such as home repairs or improvements or payment of property taxes. These loans are for low- and moderate-income seniors.
2. **Home equity conversion mortgages** (HECMs) are federally insured reverse mortgages that are backed by the U.S. Department of Housing and Urban Development.

3. **Proprietary reverse mortgages** are private loans that are backed by the companies that develop them. People use these loans when they have significantly more equity than the federally backed loans will cover. Be careful: There are many scams in the private marketplace for these loans.

The AARP has an excellent online resource that explains how reverse mortgages work. Visit *www.aarp.org/money/revmort*.

Question 60: **What are the pros of a reverse mortgage?**

The biggest pro is that your elder gets the cash she needs to continue living in her home. If your elder is on a small fixed income, tapping the equity on the home may be the only option for her to stay in that home. If she has enough equity built up, she will not be forced to sell the home to pay for health care costs and other living expenses.

Question 61: **What are the cons of a reverse mortgage?**

Costs are very high, which is the primary reason to tread carefully. The highest are the upfront costs paid from the home's equity at closing. Reverse-mortgage lenders make their money through interest, origination fees, and points. The interest rate varies according to the market, but closing costs are significantly higher with reverse mortgages. Lenders also can charge fees for servicing the loan throughout the term of the mortgage. Lenders set the fees, not the federal government.

If your elder chooses this route, she still will be responsible for real-estate taxes, conventional homeowners insurance, and home repairs, and will have to pay mortgage insurance, too. Although your senior may have plenty of equity, mortgage insurance is needed to protect the lender in case the property value falls after the reverse mortgage is made. Mortgage insurance also covers the lender if your elder lives longer than expected and accrued interest exceeds the value of the home.

If you decide that the reverse mortgage route is the best way to go for your elder, don't expect to see much cash from the property after your elder dies. The amount that is owed on the reverse mortgage grows over time. Interest is charged on the outstanding balance and added to the amount of the loan each month. Reverse mortgages can eat up all or most of the equity in a home, which means your elder will have less to leave to her heirs. According to most reverse-mortgage contracts, upon your elder's death, the home must be sold to pay off the reverse mortgage. Interest that accrues on a reverse mortgage cannot be deducted from income tax due until the loan is paid off.

In some states, a reverse mortgage also can be a barrier for qualifying for Medicaid. Be sure to talk with an attorney familiar with these rules before choosing to use a reverse mortgage. Untapped equity in a home is not included when calculating qualification for Medicaid, but a reverse mortgage becomes tapped equity in some states.

Question 62: **What happens to the home after an elder dies if a reverse mortgage is used?**

That will depend on how the reverse mortgage is structured. Be sure that you understand what will happen to the home before you even take out the reverse mortgage.

In most cases, the home must be sold to pay off the reverse mortgage. If there is equity, the remaining value will likely become part of your elder's estate.

Chapter **7**

MANAGING AND AUGMENTING YOUR ELDER'S FUNDS

YOU MAY FIND that you need to take control of your elder's funds. In this chapter, we'll consider your options for managing those funds.

Question 63: **What types of bank accounts work best for managing an elder's money?**

The best way to manage your elder's money is through a joint convenience checking account. To set up such an account, you'll need to follow the rules set by your elder's bank. As long as your state's laws authorize a joint convenience checking account, it's better to use this form of checking rather than an account with joint tenancy with right of survivor, which is your other option.

With the convenience checking account, you will be limited as a cosigner to withdrawing funds solely for the benefit of your elder. Setting up a joint convenience checking account works best if the funds put into the account are needed for routine expenditures and your elder needs assistance with routine bill paying.

Question 64: **What forms do I need to fill out to get access to certain accounts?**

This depends on the type of account and the institution holding it. But if you have not set up some form of joint checking and your elder becomes incompetent, you will need to go to court. I discuss the problems of incompetency and what you need to do if you have not planned for incompetency in Chapter 4.

Question 65: **If an elder is receiving government aid, can I supplement that income with my own money?**

If your elder is receiving Supplemental Security Income (SSI) from the federal government, you must be certain that you do not give your elder more money than is allowed based on the maximum monthly income rules in your state. Also, if your elder has qualified for Medicaid, make sure that you know the income limitations in your state.

If you exceed allowable income for either of these federal assistance programs, your elder could lose his assistance.

Question 66: **How much money can I give an elder without affecting government aid?**

The amount you will be able to give your elder will depend on the type of aid he receives and on the amount of income that he is allowed to get and still receive government aid. Those amounts vary by state, so you will need to contact the state in which your elder lives if your elder does not know the rules of his state.

Question 67: **What is the best way to give an elder money?**

If government assistance is not an issue, you are allowed to give up to $12,000 per person without having to worry about gift taxes.

If you intend to give money to both your parents, that means you can give up to $24,000 to the couple without having to worry about gift taxes. You also can avoid gift taxes by paying your elder's medical bills directly. I'll talk more about how to avoid gift taxes in Chapter 15.

Question 68: **What if my parents need money, but I can't afford to give them any?**

Only you can decide how much money you can afford to give your parents. Your primary concern must be for your nuclear family—your spouse and your children. They must come first.

Yes, it may be hard to say no to your parents, but if giving them money means that you're going to put your own family at risk of losing their home or going hungry or going without other things that they need, you must say no. Instead of giving money to your parents, give your time and efforts to help them find the financial aid they need by talking to state and local agencies that help the elderly. Visit the Administration on Aging website (*www.aoa.gov/eldfam/How_To_Find/How_To_Find.aspx*) to learn more about ways to seek help.

Question 69: **What if my parents are using guilt to get money out of me?**

You may find that your parents use guilt to try to get more money out of you than you can afford. Don't ever give money because of guilt. Your gifts of money should be because of love and should be based on what you can afford without hurting your own family.

First, you may want to call your brother or sister and find out exactly what they are doing for your parents. Your parents could be trying to play one child against another. If your siblings are in better financial shape, have a heart-to-heart with them about what's going on and about your financial position.

Once you're on the same page as your siblings, sit down and have a family meeting with everyone involved, including your parents. Review your parents' actual financial needs, and come up with a family plan that everyone can agree on. You may decide to give more time, and your siblings may decide to give more money. Making the decision as a family will help to stop the "guilt trip" games and get your parents the help they need.

Chapter **8**

DEALING WITH THE COSTS OF CARE

IF YOU THINK you had a hard time talking about finances, trying to get information about medical care and its costs may be even harder. Many people avoid talking about the details of their medical care throughout their lives and find it difficult to have to share that information when they get older—especially with their children. In this chapter, I'll review the basics of the medical coverage your elder gets from Medicare and Medicaid.

Question 70: **How do I know if my parents are telling me the truth about their medical expenses?**

You'll probably find it difficult to get a truthful answer from your elders about their medical costs. This may or may not be deliberate. Medicare can be a difficult program to sort out. Just ask to see a Medicare statement from a recent doctor visit, and you'll get an idea of the trouble your elder has trying to determine his true medical expenses.

Ask to see your elder's Medicare statements for the past few months. You can use those statements to develop a monthly estimate for out-of-pocket medical costs. Don't forget to add in the monthly amount that is deducted from your elder's check for Medicare Part

B (major medical) and Part D (prescriptions). Your elder also may have chosen a Medicare Part C (Medicare Advantage program).

Yes, this alphabet soup can be difficult to sort out. I'll take you through the Medicare basics in this chapter, but if you want to know more about the details, read my book *The Complete Idiot's Guide to Social Security and Medicare*.

Question 71: **What do I (or an elder) have to pay for, and what does the government pay?**

Every senior who has earned forty credits gets Medicare Part A (hospitalization) for free at age sixty-five. One can earn four credits for every year of work, so for people who have worked at least ten years, this is an easy hurdle. You get one credit for every $920 you earn per quarter, up to four credits per year.

Seniors also are automatically signed up for Medicare Part B (major medical), but that isn't free. In 2008, the monthly cost was $96.40; this amount has been going up 3 to 4 percent per year. If your elder wants coverage for the prescription medications he takes, he must choose a Medicare Part D plan, which costs an additional $20 to $40 per month for most seniors. Seniors choose this plan from about forty plans available in most states (the number varies by state). Seniors also can choose a Medicare Advantage plan, which sometimes covers both major medical and prescription needs, depending on the plan. In my answers to questions 72 through 83, I'll cover more details about what your elder pays and what the government pays.

Question 72: **What does Medicare pay?**

As I mentioned earlier, your elder likely has Medicare Part A, Medicare Part B, and Medicare Part D. In my answer to Question 79, I'll talk about Medicare Advantage, which is the private Medicare option. Let's take a closer look at Medicare parts A and B. I'll cover Medicare Part D in my answers to questions 75 and 76.

Medicare Part A is essentially the in-patient portion of Medicare. Coverage includes hospital stays, care in skilled nursing facilities, home health care after being released from a hospital, and hospice care. In the hospital or a skilled nursing facility, your elder's Medicare coverage includes a semiprivate room, meals, general nursing, and other hospital services and supplies. Part A does not cover private-duty nursing or a television or telephone in the room. You also can't get coverage for a private room unless it is medically necessary.

If your elder does need a skilled nursing facility, he must go directly from a three-day hospital stay to the nursing home. People who have been diagnosed with a terminal illness can get hospice care from a Medicare-approved hospice, including drugs for symptom control and pain relief and other services not otherwise covered by Medicare. Hospice care frequently can be given in your elder's home. However, short-term hospital and inpatient respite care also may be possible when needed.

You've probably already guessed that Part A does not cover 100 percent of your costs. You will have to pay both a deductible and coinsurance for each stay in a hospital. Before we get into your costs, I first must explain something unique to Medicare, called benefit periods.

Medicare uses benefit periods to track your use of hospitals and skilled nursing facilities. A benefit period begins when you enter a hospital or skilled nursing facility. It ends when you haven't received hospital or skilled nursing care for sixty days. As long as you are out of hospital or skilled nursing care for sixty days, a new benefit period begins. There is no limit to the number of new benefit periods you can have.

Why are benefit periods so important? Because each benefit period requires that you pay a new inpatient deductible, which was $1,024 in 2008. Coinsurance also is affected by the benefit periods. In 2008, coinsurance for an inpatient hospital stay was $256 a day for the 61st to 90th day of each benefit period. Coinsurance then jumps to $512 a day for the 91st to 150th day, which would be covered under the provision for lifetime reserve days.

You are responsible for all costs after the 150th day. Deductibles and coinsurance rates are set each year by Medicare.

Part B is essentially your elder's medical insurance. The deductible for 2008 for Part B was $135. A copayment of 20 percent is required for most Medicare-approved services and equipment under Part B, but there is a 50 percent copayment for outpatient mental health care.

Question 73: What doesn't Medicare pay?

In addition to the copays and deductibles that your elder must pay out of pocket, as discussed in Question 72, Medicare does not pay for long-term care. Once your elder needs more than 150 days of care, his Medicare coverage is maxed out. Any longer-term care would need to be paid by a long-term-care policy, or your elder would need to qualify for aid through Medicaid. Medicare also pays very little for home health care for a very limited time.

Question 74: What options does a person have to cover the costs not covered by Medicare?

Your elder has several options to consider to pay for costs not covered by Medicare:

- **Medigap policy**—These policies close the gaps for copays and deductibles not paid by Medicare.
- **Medicare Advantage**—These are private Medicare programs that provide coverage with lower or no copays or deductibles, but be sure you know what your elder will be paying out of pocket. Sometimes doctor costs are lower and hospital costs are higher.
- **Long-term-care insurance**—These policies help to pay the costs of long-term care and home health care when Medicare runs out.
- **Medicaid**—This is a government program for low-income seniors who can't afford to pay for long-term care. I'll talk

more about qualifying for this program in my answer to Question 81.

Question 75: **How much does an elder pay for the new Medicare prescription drug plan?**

The amount your elder pays for the new Medicare prescription drug plan varies greatly state by state. Within each state, your elder usually will find about forty plans available on the market. Your best bet to find out more about the plans offered in your state is to go to *www.medicare.gov* and use the tool for locating Medicare Part D plans. Most plans range in cost from $20 to $40 per month.

Question 76: **What's covered under the new Medicare prescription drug plan?**

That's not an easy question to answer because it depends on the private plan your elder has chosen, but here are the basics of what is supposed to be offered:

- Your elder may have to pay a deductible (which was $275 in 2008), which means that your elder will have to spend $275 on drugs before drug costs will be covered under the plan. Some plans are sold without this deductible.
- Once the deductible is met, your elder will pay 25 percent of prescription costs, and the insurer will pay 75 percent of the costs. The 25 percent is the senior's copay. The payment scheme continues until your elder spends $500 out of pocket on drugs and receives $2,510 in drugs. Copays vary depending on the private plan chosen.
- Your elder then loses all coverage until he spends another $3,850 on drugs. This is what people call the donut hole because seniors must pay for 100 percent of the cost of their drugs at this point.

■ Once your elder spends $4,050 out of pocket, then he will pay only 5 percent of all future drug costs, and the insurer will pay 95 percent. The amount to be paid out of pocket will be adjusted yearly.

If this isn't confusing enough, there are a lot more options from which you can choose. That's because Congress decided to make this plan available through private insurers rather than directly from Medicare. Insurers were given great flexibility in how they could design their plans, provided that they met the minimum requirements I just outlined. Insurers came up with many alternatives to this design.

Question 77: **What's not covered under the new Medicare prescription drug plan?**

That's not an easy question to answer, because it depends on the private program your elder picked. Every plan has a formulary that lists the drugs to be covered and even groups these drugs into tiers. The private plan pays a different amount depending on the tier in which each drug falls. In addition, plans can limit your elder's drug use and require prior authorization for some drugs. They also can limit the quantity your elder can take and require your elder to try cheaper medication before he's allowed to take the medication that his doctor prefers.

Question 78: **What are the different types of Medigap policies?**

You can choose among ten plans lettered from A to J. Coverage varies depending on how much and what you want to pay for, but each plan must include the following:

■ Hospital coinsurance (see Question 72 for full details about these costs)

- Full coverage for 365 additional hospital days (after Medicare hospital reserve days are exhausted)
- Twenty percent copayment for physician and other Part B services
- Cost of three pints of blood

In addition, some popular options you can shop for include:

- Coverage of Medicare hospital deductible
- Skilled nursing facility daily coinsurance
- Coverage of Part B $124 deductible
- Coverage while traveling outside the United States (it's available for only the first two months of a trip)
- Coverage of doctors' fees that exceed the Medicare approved charge
- Medically necessary home care costs not paid by Medicare

There are some things for which coverage simply isn't available. These include custodial care (such as feeding, bathing, and grooming) either at home or in a nursing home, long-term skilled care in a nursing home, unlimited prescription drugs, vision care, dental care, and a private nurse.

Question 79: **What is Medicare Advantage, and what does it cover?**

Medicare Advantage plans are plans your elder buys from a private insurance company instead of traditional Medicare. In order to qualify for a Medicare Advantage plan, your elder must have Medicare Part A and Medicare Part B. There are several types of Medicare Advantage plans, and each plan's coverage must at least match the coverage offered by traditional Medicare. Medicare Advantage options include:

- **Medicare health maintenance organizations (HMOs)—** If your elder chooses this type of plan, he can use only doctors, hospitals, and other providers in the HMO network. He chooses a primary care doctor, who decides when he should see a specialist and which specialist he can see. Neither Medicare nor the HMO will pay for unauthorized visits to specialists. They also will not pay for visits to medical providers outside the plan. If you pay additional premiums, some HMOs do offer partial coverage for point-of-service (POS) benefits outside the plan, which means your elder can choose his own doctors, but he'll pay more.

- **Medicare preferred provider organizations (PPOs)**— Although similar to HMOs, PPOs offer more flexibility. Your elder's reimbursement for medical care will be higher if he sees in-network doctors, but he can get reimbursed for care from doctors or hospitals outside the network, as well. He doesn't have to see a primary care physician before being permitted to contact a specialist. Premiums are higher for the increased flexibility.

- **Provider-sponsored organizations (PSOs)**—PSOs are ventures owned and sponsored by medical providers. They operate much as HMOs do. The big difference is that rather than being owned and managed by an insurer, they are owned and managed by a medical-provider group (which can include doctors, laboratories, and hospitals). PSOs are new to the Medicare system and have different rules in different states.

- **Private fee-for-service plans (PFFS)**—These plans work much like traditional Medicare. Your elder pays an initial premium for the plan, plus deductibles and copayments.

- **Medical savings accounts (MSAs)**—Your elder can choose to save for his own medical costs in tax-advantaged medical savings accounts. With this option, your elder buys a high-deductible insurance plan (usually with a deductible of $1,000 to $3,000) and pays all medical costs up to that deductible.

Question 80: **What are an elder's options for covering long-term care?**

Your elder has several options to consider for long-term care. Here's a brief overview of each:

- **Long-term-care insurance**—Your elder will need to choose among several key coverage options. The most important is how long he wants his coverage to last. Options vary from one to six years. Next, your elder will need to select an elimination period; his coverage won't start until the end of the elimination period. Ninety days is common, since Medicare does cover costs prior to that time. Your elder also will need to choose a coverage amount, which usually ranges from $1,000 to $6,000 per month. Most plans also have lifetime caps, which can be as low as $36,000 and as high as $1 million.
- **Continuous-care community**—These communities are designed for people who want to age in one place. Your elder would start out in an independent home or apartment and then as his care needs changed, he would move to an assisted-living facility or a nursing home. If your elder chooses this option, make sure that you have an attorney carefully review the contracts to ensure that your elder will have the long-term care he may need.
- **Medicaid planning**—Many families plan for Medicaid qualification. This can be a tricky situation, so be sure that you've chosen an attorney who knows how to prevent problems with the government.

Question 81: **Who qualifies for Medicaid?**

Qualifications for Medicaid vary by state, even though it is a federal and state program that pays for some or all of the following services:

- Physicians' visits
- Inpatient and outpatient hospital services
- Prescriptions
- Mental health care
- Home- and community-based care
- Transportation to medical appointments
- Nursing home care

Your elder automatically qualifies for Medicaid if he is a recipient of Supplemental Security Income (SSI) or an Old Age Pension (OAP). If he doesn't have SSI or OAP, he can apply when in need of intensive in-home or nursing home care.

In order for your elder to apply for Medicaid, he will need the following items:

- Social Security card
- Latest checking and savings account statements (or passbook)
- Current rent receipt or home property tax statement
- Car or truck registration
- Any life insurance policies
- Proof of earnings if working
- Proof of income from sources such as pension, veterans benefits, and interest from investments, rentals, or loans
- Proof of age (birth or baptismal certificate)
- Proof of U.S. citizenship (birth certificate) or alien registration card
- State-issued ID card or driver's license

If both your parents are alive, you must submit this information for both of them, not just the one who needs help.

In order to get help, your elder must meet the requirements for help with activities of daily living, which include getting out of bed, using a toilet, walking, dressing, bathing, caring for teeth, eating, preparing meals, doing housework and laundry, shopping, managing medicine, making and going to appointments, managing money, arranging for services, and using a phone.

In addition to meeting the requirements for help with activities, your elder must meet the financial criteria, which include a monthly income lower than mandated by the state (you'll need to contact your state for its income qualifications) and resources amounting to less than $2,000 ($3,000 for couples). Some resources are exempt. These include:

- The home in which the applicant or spouse resides or to which the applicant intends to return
- A car valued below $4,650 or of any value if used for medical transportation
- Personal belongings, such as clothing and furniture, valued at less than $2,000
- Term life insurance
- Irrevocable burial policy

All of the following resources *will* count when assessing a person's financial needs:

- Checking and savings accounts
- Stocks, bonds, and other investments
- Rental property/land and vacation homes
- Recreational vehicles
- Whole life insurance and revocable burial policies

If your elder is married and has more than $2,000 in resources, the spouse may be eligible for spousal protection, but may need to spend down resources. If you want to apply for Medicaid for one of your parents and the other is still alive, don't try to get through the process without the help of an attorney who is used to working with Medicaid issues.

Question 82: **Is a nursing home legally obligated to care for my parent twenty-four hours a day?**

Yes, if your elder has been placed in a nursing home for medical reasons, the nursing home is required to care for your elder twenty-four hours a day. If you believe that care has not been adequate, contact the state agency that monitors nursing homes, and file a complaint.

Question 83: **Can I pay extra to have someone spend one-on-one time with an elder?**

You can pay extra for an aide or nurse to spend one-on-one time with your elder as long as your elder is not receiving help from Medicaid. If your elder does have Medicaid coverage, be sure to check on your state's rules. In many states, your elder could lose his Medicaid coverage if family members show that they are able to pay for care.

Chapter 9

BASICS OF ESTATE PLANNING

YOU MAY HESITATE to discuss estate planning with your elder because you've never really talked about your elder's financial position. Get over this hesitation. There is nothing worse than dying without a will and proper estate planning.

When one dies without a will, the state decides how to divvy up the money. So, do take the initiative to be sure that your elder has discussed estate planning with her attorney, even if you don't feel comfortable getting into the specifics or your elder doesn't want to talk about them with you. Even if there isn't a lot of money involved, your elder should sit down with an attorney to be sure that her wishes will be carried out. In this chapter, I'll review the key estate-planning items your elder should consider.

Question 84: **What is estate planning?**

Estate planning is the process of determining what your elder wants to happen to her estate, which includes all the rights, titles, and interests that your elder has in the property she owns. When preparing a plan, your elder should consider the accumulation of that property, how she wants to conserve its value, and, finally, how she wants to distribute her estate after her death. Throughout this process, consider the best ways to effectively and efficiently accomplish these tasks, keeping both tax and nontax objectives in mind. Estate planning and financial planning involve many of the same concerns, including income tax planning, investment planning, insurance planning, and retirement planning. There are three main objectives of estate planning:

1. Preserve the wealth that has been passed down through previous generations.
2. Use the wealth as desired during one's lifetime.
3. Pass on to one's heirs the greatest possible amount of that wealth in the appropriate form after one's death.

There are several key words that are unique to estate planning. I will present them in greater detail later, but I want to introduce them here:

- Probate is the process of proving who is entitled to get the property if the person who died did not make that clear before her death.
- Testator (male) and testatrix (female) refer to people who leave a valid will upon death.
- Intestacy is what an estate is called if there is no will. Partial intestacy means the will did not effectively dispose of all the assets.

Three types of property classifications are generally used in estate planning:

- Real property includes land and any permanent improvements on that land.
- Tangible personal property includes property other than real estate that has a value because of its physical existence. This includes such things as cars, furniture, and collectibles.
- Intangible personal property includes property that can't be touched but that has a value because of the legal rights

held. This can include a stock certificate or an installment note, but it also can include copyrights, patents, and other intellectual property rights.

Question 85: **Who needs estate planning?**

Just about everyone. Even though your elder may not be wealthy, some degree of planning will probably be necessary. Here are a few examples:

People with minor children—If your elder has responsibility for minor children, she needs to specify who will care for the children upon her death and how she will provide for that care financially. One normally makes these provisions in a will.

People who own assets in multiple states—Estate planning will prevent what is called ancillary probate, in which an additional probate process must be completed in a state different from the one in which your elder resided because she owned real estate in that second state. Ancillary probate can be very costly and can reduce the value of your elder's estate.

People who own a small business—Your elder must determine what should be done with her interest in that business, whether it is to be passed on to her heirs or sold. If it is to be sold, your elder must be certain that her interest in the estate will be marketable at the time of her death.

People who will have to pay estate taxes—If your elder's estate is large enough that taxes will need to be paid upon her death, your elder must plan for that payment. Your elder should be sure that there are enough liquid assets to avoid the forced sale of estate assets. Often this is done with life insurance planning.

People who want to determine how their assets will be divided among their heirs—If your elder doesn't specify how she wants to divide her assets, the state will do so as part of probate.

People in high-liability occupations—If your elder is in an occupation that carries a high risk of being sued or facing claims from creditors, estate planning will help protect assets. Doctors are prime candidates for this type of planning.

People whose spouses are not U.S. citizens—If your elder's spouse is not a U.S. citizen, she will need to provide for a noncitizen spouse's death. In most cases, the marital deduction is not available for a spouse who is not a U.S. citizen.

People who think they may become disabled—If your elder thinks she may become disabled, she needs to appoint a surrogate decision-maker as part of estate planning. A surrogate will be able to make medical and financial decisions. Your elder also may need to plan for possible Medicaid eligibility as part of her estate-planning process.

Question 86: What are the financial goals of estate planning?

There are two types of financial goals: nontax financial goals and tax-related financial goals. Here, I'll focus on the nontax goals, which will involve issues such as preserving a business's value, maximizing an estate's financial flexibility, maximizing benefits to a surviving spouse, minimizing nontax transfer costs, and main-taining adequate liquidity. Tax-related financial goals focus on how to minimize your elder's estate-tax bite, including:

- **Preserving a business's value**—Without proper planning, the value of a business could plummet after your elder's death. Maintain the value of the business by using buy-sell agreements among the owners that lay out the distribu-tion of the business upon one owner's death. Usually, these agreements are funded with life insurance policies.
- **Maximizing your elder's estate flexibility**—The key to keeping an estate's flexibility is to make it as easy as possible for your elder's heirs to access the liquid assets after your elder dies by using certain types of trusts (see Chapter 11), payable-on-death (POD) designations for bank accounts,

and transfer-on-death (TOD) designations for brokerage accounts.

- **Maximizing benefits for the surviving spouse**—The best way to ensure that your elder's spouse won't be socked with a lot of taxes upon his death is to place the spouse's estate in a trust that gives the surviving spouse access to both the income and principal of the trust.

- **Minimizing nontax transfer costs**—One way to minimize the costs associated with your elder's estate planning is to use will substitutes, such as taking a title to property with joint tenancy with right of survivorship. This will allow your elder to avoid the costs of setting up a trust.

- **Maintaining adequate liquidity**—Your elder must plan for enough cash and cash equivalents as part of her estate to cover all the immediate nontax and tax costs of settling the estate. Cash equivalents can include money market accounts, IRAs, and other investments that can be easily converted to cash. Cash needs after an elder's death are most commonly met with life insurance policies.

Question 87: What are the nonfinancial goals of estate planning?

The nonfinancial goals focus on several issues: meeting the needs of dependents, properly distributing assets, and controlling one's assets after one's death. When considering the needs of dependents, the amount of planning will depend on the degree of support each dependent will need. For example, a minor child who can be expected to attain full capabilities when she reaches adulthood will need less planning than a disabled child who will need planning for the basics of life. If applicable, your elder will need to specify who will be responsible for a disabled child's clothing, food, and medical care.

Proper distribution of assets involves more than just deciding who gets what. Your elder also must decide the most efficient way to transfer the assets, so the transfer can be done as quickly and expediently as possible.

Another key nonfinancial goal is control. With a properly drawn will, your elder can be certain that her assets will go to the people she intends to get them.

Question 88: **What are the tax goals of estate planning?**

These goals will depend on the type of tax involved. Tax goals are grouped into two pots: one for income taxes and the second for transfer taxes, which include gift, estate, and generation-skipping taxes. Tax goals related to income tax involve minimizing taxes through shifting the receipt of income, shifting the taxation of income, and deferring the recognition of income and gain. Tax goals related to the various transfer taxes involve freezing or reducing the value of assets subject to tax; using exclusions, exemptions, deductions, and credits; and delaying the payment of taxes. Chapters 12 through 15 focus on these tax questions.

Chapter **10**

TO HAVE A WILL OR NOT

As I **DISCUSSED** in Chapter 9, it's critical for your elder to sit down and discuss estate planning with an attorney, as well as to draw up a will. In this chapter, I will take a closer look at the provisions of a will.

Question 89: **What is a will?**

The primary purpose of a will is to make provisions for how your elder wants to dispose of any property after his death. There are several different types of wills:

- Simple (or single) will—This type of will involves a single document with provisions executed by a single maker.
- Joint will—This type of will involves a single document with provisions executed by more than one party. It is most commonly used by a husband and wife.
- Mutual will—This type of will involves a single or multiple documents executed by two or more parties. The parties contract with each other to leave their property in a specified manner.
- Reciprocal will—This is a type of mutual will in which each party names the other as the recipient of his or her property.

Although there are several different types of wills, financial planners exclusively recommend the use of simple wills. All other types of wills can make it impossible for a surviving party to make changes in his estate planning after the death of a party to the will.

Question 90: **What are the requirements for a valid will?**

To be valid, all wills must meet certain basic requirements. These include:

Minimum age—The person writing the will must be of legal age to write a valid will. That age is eighteen or nineteen in most states.

Testamentary capacity—A person who makes a will, a testator (if male) or a testatrix (if female), must have the testamentary capacity to make the will. This involves three elements:

1. The will maker must understand the nature of the document he is signing.
2. The will maker must understand the nature and extent of his property.
3. The will maker must understand who is in his family.

The term "of sound mind and body" captures the most important elements of testamentary capacity.

Valid form—The will must be in a form that is recognized as valid in the state in which it will be executed. Every state authorizes a typewritten or witnessed will, but some people like to be more creative. If your elder wants to use another form of will, be sure that it will be recognized as valid in your state.

Properly executed—Every state has requirements about how the will should be executed. Be sure that you know the requirements for the state in which your elder resides, and follow them exactly.

Question 91: **What are the typical clauses of a will?**

Common wills are broken down into four types of clauses: preliminary clauses, dispositive clauses, appointment clauses, and concluding clauses.

1. Preliminary clauses set the stage for the will with identifying information, including the name of the maker, the maker's residence, the fact that this is meant to be the maker's will, and the revocation of any prior wills.
2. Dispositive clauses specify who should get the assets.
3. Appointment clauses specify the personal representative and his fiduciary responsibilities, as well as any guardianships.
4. Concluding clauses seal the validity of the will, including signatures of the maker and required witnesses.

Question 92: **What are dispositive clauses of a will?**

The dispositive clauses are the core of the will, where the maker specifies how his assets will be distributed. Hopefully, your elder will write his will long before his death; in that case, the actual property owned at the time of death may be different from that owned at the time the will was written. Specific property items are seldom mentioned in the will unless they are family heirlooms or other assets that will definitely be there at the time of death.

These clauses should be written with a clear command of how the property should be distributed. If the words *wish* or *hope* are included, the court may decide not to honor those wishes or hopes. Real property is disposed by a *devise*, and the recipient is known as the *devisee*. Personal property is disposed as a *bequest* or *legacy*, and the recipient is a *legatee*. If the assets to be disposed are specifically named, then it's a *specific bequest*. If the bequest is to be paid out of the general assets, then it's a *general bequest*.

If your elder has many small items to list in the will that are not of great value, include a *tangible personal property clause* that will list the items and to whom they should go. Some states allow people to dispose of small items by including a document called a *tangible personal property memorandum*, which is separate from the will. The advantage of the memorandum is that since it is not part of the will, if your elder wants to change it, he doesn't have to go to the expense of executing a new will.

Your elder may not want to give the asset directly to the beneficiary but instead transfer the property to a testamentary trust. If that's the case, the will also should include terms for how the trust must be distributed. If the trust already exists and will be added to at the time of your elder's death, then it's known as a *pour-over trust*, and the will is a *pour-over will*. I'll talk more about trusts in Chapter 16.

In all cases, the will should name both a primary beneficiary (first priority) and contingent beneficiary (who gets the assets if the primary beneficiary is not alive) for each asset named in the will. This will prevent any problems in the event that a beneficiary dies before your elder does.

Question 93: **What are appointment clauses of a will?**

The most important appointment clause in any will is the clause that specifies the personal representative. Question 97 explains who the personal representative is and briefly describes his or her duties.

In addition to appointing a personal representative to administer your elder's will, your elder also may need to appoint guardians. For example, if your elder has guardianship responsibility for children who are minors, he should specify who he wants to be the guardian and conservator of the minor children. Your elder may specify a guardian and conservator for favorite pets, as well.

Your elder also may want to include a fiduciary powers clause that specifies the powers he wants to give appointees. If your elder doesn't include this clause, the appointees will be able to do only what is specified by state statute.

Question 94: **What are concluding clauses of a will?**

The first of the concluding clauses reaffirms that the document is a person's last will and testament and includes your elder's signature and the date that he signed the document. That clause is followed by the attestation (statement of witnesses) clause. The witnesses affirm that they saw your elder sign the will and that your elder had testamentary capacity at the time of signing (that is, your elder was "of sound mind and body"). This clause should include all the essential statements that the witnesses would have to verify if they were called to personally testify at the time of probate. If so, this also can serve as a self-proving clause, which means that the proof that the will is valid can be assumed and the courts won't need to talk with the witnesses.

Both your elder's signature and the signatures of the witnesses must be notarized. If your elder's state does allow the attestation clause to be admitted to probate court without personal testimony, be sure that your elder's concluding clauses are done in the form specified by state statute.

Question 95: **What is a no-contest clause in a will?**

If your elder wants to leave someone out of his will, be sure to include a no-contest clause. This type of clause usually specifies that if your elder wants to disinherit a family member but that family member successfully challenges the provision in the will that disinherits him, then the family member receives only a nominal amount that your elder specifies, such as one dollar. This clause also can state that if a beneficiary contests the inheritance because he is not happy with the amount received, then that amount is revoked and distributed as if that beneficiary had died before the testator or testatrix.

Probate judges may not enforce a no-contest clause because it takes away the right of a family member to legally contest the will. Some states have statutes regarding how no-contest laws should be treated by the probate court.

Question 96: **What are other common optional clauses in a will?**

Other common clauses specify disposition of assets or payment of taxes. If your elder anticipates that there will be estate taxes, your elder may want to include a clause specifying how those taxes should be paid. If your elder has intangible property, such as a copyright or patent, he may want to include an intangible personal property clause to specify who will control those rights. If your elder has many different parcels of real estate, he may want to include a real-property clause to specify the disposition of the property. To ensure that all property is disposed of, even if not specifically named in the will, your elder may want to include a residuary clause that disposes of all probate property not effectively disposed of in other clauses of the will.

Question 97: **Who is a personal representative, and what are his or her duties?**

When drafting a will, your elder must designate a personal representative who will carry out his wishes after his death. In most states, this personal representative is called an *executor* (if male) or *executrix* (if female). If a person dies without a will, the state will appoint a personal representative, who can be called an *administrator* (if male) or an *administratix* (if female).

If your elder appoints a personal representative in his will, the probate court will likely honor his wishes unless it finds a good reason to deny them, such as the court finds a personal representative to be untrustworthy. If your elder does not appoint a personal representative or if your elder dies without a will, then the state appoints a personal representative for your elder based on state statutes. State statutes specify a priority list of people who can be appointed as personal representatives. First priority goes to a surviving spouse, then adult children of the deceased, and so on. If the state can't find an appropriate relative, an attorney or bank will be appointed to handle probate.

The key duties of the personal representative include:

- Collecting money in bank accounts titled solely in the decedent's name
- Notifying all financial institutions that any communications about the decedent's assets should be sent to the personal representative
- Collecting any money due to the decedent, such as rents, payments, salary or wages, or life insurance policies
- Paying any money due to valid creditors of the deceased
- Paying all taxes due
- Managing estate assets during the probate process
- Distributing any estate assets left after the payment of all valid creditors and all taxes

Question 98: **How does a person amend or revoke a will?**

All wills are totally revocable until a person's death. Each state has its own laws specifying how a person can amend or revoke a will. If your elder wants to change his will, be sure to follow the rules of his state to avoid any problems during probate. If your elder wants to revoke a will, the best way to ensure that it is never used is to collect all the copies and destroy them. If that is not possible, keep the original and have him write the word *revoked* on the front of it.

If your elder wants to revoke a will, be sure that a new will has already been executed. If your elder doesn't do this and he dies before the new will is completed, the court will consider that he died intestate (without a will), and the state will determine how his assets should be distributed.

Question 99: **What happens if a person doesn't have a will when he dies?**

Some people can't even think about their death, so they never prepare a will. Others prepare a will, but it does not dispose of all assets effectively. If a person dies without a valid will, he is said to die *intestate*, and the state laws of intestate succession take over. Each state has its own set of laws to deal with intestate succession, and the probate proceedings are called intestacy proceedings.

Sometimes a person will die in partial intestacy, with only some of his assets not properly disposed of in a will. Avoid this by including a residuary clause, which specifies the disposition of leftover assets.

A person who has no valid will and has property not held in a will-substitute form, such as property titled joint tenancy with right of survivorship, is said to die in total intestacy. When this happens, the state laws determine what goes to whom, and the state appoints a personal representative for the deceased. (Question 97 covers the duties of the personal representative.) To avoid intestacy proceedings and all the problems that can arise, be sure to encourage your elder to write a will.

Question 100: **What provisions are made for survivors when no will exists?**

Surviving family members have first priority. The states believe that the decedent's spouse and lineal descendents (children, grandchildren, great-grandchildren, adopted children, and illegitimate children) should get most of the deceased's property. Before the state will even consider the rights of more remote family members, the spouse and lineal descendents must be cared for appropriately. The proportion of the estate that goes to the eligible family members is specified by state law.

Question 101: **How is the estate distributed if a person dies intestate?**

After the payment of all claims by creditors and any taxes due, the estate will start distribution of the assets by giving the spouse his or her share as stated in the intestacy statute. This could be the entire estate if there are no lineal descendants. In some states, the spouse may get all the assets even if there are surviving lineal descendants, if these descendants are also the descendants of the surviving spouse. Each state has its own laws, so if your elder wants to have some control over the distribution of his assets, your elder must make a valid will.

Question 102: **What are the disadvantages of intestacy?**

There are many disadvantages of intestacy. The only advantage is that your elder doesn't have to deal with what happens after he dies. Here are some important disadvantages:

- Intestacy laws as written in each state must be applied rigidly. There are no provisions for special needs. For example, if your elder has a disabled child and wants to set aside a larger share for his or her care, the state laws won't allow for that special circumstance if your elder dies intestate.
- The share each heir gets is set by law, so the assets will not be distributed based on what your elder thinks is best for each heir.
- All children are treated equally, regardless of age or competency.
- If your elder has guardianship over minor children, a guardian or conservator will be appointed by the court, and it may be someone your elder would not have wanted to be in charge of his children.
- Most states have no provisions for domestic partners or other nonfamily members.
- No state has provisions to give part of your elder's estate to charity.
- Estate taxes could be higher because the property will be distributed by state law, and that distribution may not minimize the tax bite.

■ The state will name your elder's personal representative, who will administer the disposition of his assets.

Don't let your elder die intestate. Encourage him to take the time to prepare a valid will, so he can be sure that his assets will be disposed of in the way that he wants.

Chapter **11**

DEALING WITH PROBATE

AFTER YOUR ELDER'S death, any property he owns needs to be distributed appropriately. Even if your elder does have a will, his personal representative will need to complete a process called probate before disposing of your elder's assets. This chapter reviews the basics of probate and the statures that affect the disposition of your elder's assets after death.

Question 103: **What is probate?**

You've probably heard the most difficult process after a person's death is probate. *Probate* is derived from a Latin word that means "to prove." In probate, you must go before a judge to prove that the will is valid. You must be able to prove several key things:

- The document you present is the will that your elder intended to be presented as his last will and testament.
- The person whose will you are presenting is dead.
- The will you are presenting has not been revoked.
- The will was properly executed and was valid in the state in which it was executed.

Each state has its own laws about probate, but in most cases, you can prove these things using an affidavit by the person appointed in the will as the deceased person's personal representative. That representative is called an *executor*, if male, or *executrix*, if female.

If the person died without a will or with a will found to be invalid or incomplete, some additional issues must be investigated and established during probate in most states:

- Was the deceased married and survived by his spouse?
- Was the deceased survived by lineal descendants (children, grandchildren, great-grandchildren, and stepchildren)?
- Were the children also the lineal descendants of the surviving spouse?
- Does the deceased have lineal descendants who are not the lineal descendants of the surviving spouse?

Question 104: **What property interests are affected by probate?**

Whether probate after your elder's death will affect property he owns depends upon how he took title to that property. If he took title in the form of "joint tenancy with right of survivorship" or "tenancy by the entirety," then he has probably designated who the owner of the property should be upon his death, and the property will not need to go through probate.

If your elder took title to the property in the form of "sole" owner, "tenancy in common," or "traditional community property," he will need to designate in his will who should get the property because it becomes part of his probate estate, and it will need to go through the probate process.

Question 105: **What are the objectives and processes of probate?**

After a person dies, his assets are distributed in a process called probate. There are three objectives of the probate process:

1. To distribute the property according to the provisions of the will
2. To pay the legitimate claims of creditors
3. To collect taxes on the estate

A probate judge, whose job it is to make sure that the three objectives are met, controls the process. First, the assets of the estate must be pulled together and secured. Then an inventory of the assets is filed with the judge. Creditors must be notified by mail, and a notice must be published in an appropriate public place, such as a newspaper where probate notices are generally published. Any valid debts, expenses, and taxes must be paid before the probate assets can be distributed to the heirs. Once all is done to the satisfaction of the judge, the assets can be distributed.

Each of these steps must be done within time frames set by the court. This ensures that the person who has been appointed as a personal representative of the decedent cannot drag her feet and delay the process indefinitely. Also the judge makes sure the property is being disposed of in a trustworthy manner and that proper records are kept of how the money is used (to pay creditors or taxes) and distributed.

Question 106: **What are the advantages of probate?**

Although many people dread the thought of going through the probate process, it does have advantages:

- **It's orderly.** A neutral party, the probate judge, oversees the collection of the assets, development of the inventory, notification of the creditors, payments to creditors and tax collectors, and the disbursement of the assets to the heirs. If the personal representative does not have strong skills in this area, the judge can be essential.
- **It's open to all parties.** Probate can serve as a forum if there are any disputes or critical issues to be decided. Beneficiaries can be certain that they will receive inherited

property with a valid title. They also can be sure that what they receive cannot be claimed by creditors or by tax collectors. Creditors can be assured of a process for payment of valid claims. Government agencies can ensure that they'll get their share in taxes.

- **It's fair**. The probate judge serves as a disinterested, unbiased arbiter of any disputes. The judge can be particularly important if someone questions the validity of the will or the specified distribution of assets.

Question 107: **What are the disadvantages of probate?**

Although there are significant advantages to probate, there are disadvantages as well:

- **It's costly**. When taking an estate through probate, everyone wants a share of the pie. Payments are usually made to an attorney, an accountant, appraisers, auctioneers, and the personal representative.
- **It's lengthy**. The actual length of time will depend on the complexity of the estate to be settled. The process can take years. For example, if a small business is involved and estate taxes are more than can be paid at the time of the death, they can be paid in installments over as long as fifteen years. The estate is open for that long, and estate assets cannot be distributed until all taxes are paid. To avoid this problem, many small-business owners take life insurance to pay the anticipated estate taxes.
- **It's public**. In most cases, personal estate information is open for public inspection.

Question 108: **How can an elder avoid probate?**

Luckily every state offers some ways to avoid probate for major assets, so your family doesn't have to wait for the probate process to be completed to make use of or dispose of those assets after your elder's death. Since probate can take a year or more, this can be a huge benefit when dealing with a home or other key assets.

When property is involved, one can own that property with a title that names the survivor's rights. These types of titles automatically transfer the property to the joint owner when one of the owners dies.

Another common way to avoid probate is to name a beneficiary when one purchases the asset or insurance policy. This type of will substitute is commonly used to avoid probate when people open accounts with banks, brokerage houses, or mutual funds, or when they buy an insurance policy.

Question 109: **What are rights of survivorship?**

Two types of property titles offer the right of survivorship. The most commonly used are joint tenancy with the right of survivorship (JTWROS) and tenancy by the entirety (TBE). The first type, JTWROS, means all owners of the property own an equal and undivided share of the property. When one of the owners dies, the property ownership automatically transfers to all other owners. This type of ownership does avoid probate but can be a problem when the last surviving owner dies. At that time, the property needs to go through probate.

Only a married couple can use TBE. Neither spouse can sell or take a loan on the property without the other spouse's permission. After the death of one spouse, the property automatically transfers to the surviving spouse; there is no probate. The property will have to go through probate after the death of the sole surviving spouse.

Question 110: **What is joint tenancy?**

Anytime two or more people share ownership in real-estate property or other assets such as a bank account, when one owner dies, that property can transfer automatically to the surviving owners without the need for a will or probate. For example, if your elder opens a bank account with one of his children as joint tenants, the child on the account can become full owner automatically without the need for a designation in your elder's will.

There are actually three types of joint bank accounts:

1. **Joint tenancy with immediate vesting**—Each owner has an immediate right to half the account but cannot withdraw more without letting the other owner know.
2. **Revocable account**—Either owner can withdraw all the funds in the account without seeking permission of the other, so neither owner's interest is vested.
3. **Convenience account**—One person deposits all the money, and a second person serves as an agent for managing the funds. The person who deposited the money has sole rights to the funds. This type of account is typically used by a child who is assisting an elderly, incapacitated parent.

Question 111: **What is a beneficiary?**

A beneficiary is any person or organization that has the legal right to receive assets or other benefits through a legal document, such as a will, trust, or insurance policy. Many types of will substitutes can be used to designate a beneficiary and avoid probate:

- Government savings bonds
- Payable-on-death (POD) accounts
- Bank account trusts or Totten trusts
- Transfer-on-death (TOD) accounts
- Contract provisions in pensions, IRAs, annuities, and life insurance policies
- Gifts causa mortis
- Revocable living trusts
- Irrevocable living trusts

Question 112: **How can a government savings bond be used as a will substitute?**

To use a government savings bond as a will substitute, your elder will need to buy Series EE bonds. He can buy these bonds using either a right-of-survivorship designation or a beneficiary designation. If your elder chooses a right-of-survivorship designation, then your elder and someone else buy the bonds as co-owners, and the surviving owner gets the proceeds upon the death of the other owner without having to go through probate. If your elder chooses a beneficiary designation, he controls the bonds completely and can change the beneficiary at any time before his death. Upon your elder's death, the beneficiary would get the proceeds without having to go through probate.

If your elder has property to leave, he can't use bonds as a will substitute. Bonds can be used as long as one can name a beneficiary or buy them with right of survivorship. For example, a father and son buy bonds with right of survivorship. When the father dies, the son gets full possession of the bonds without having to go through probate. Or a husband and wife buy bonds and name their children as beneficiaries. The children can get the bonds when their parents die without have to go through probate.

Question 113: **How can a POD account be used as a will substitute?**

When your elder opens a payable-on-death account, he maintains complete control of those funds while he is still alive. Any assets left in that account after your elder's death are then transferred to his designated beneficiary without the need for a will or probate. Beneficiaries are usually spouses, children, or charitable organizations.

Question 114: **What are Totten trusts?**

If your elder wants to use a Totten trust, he deposits the money in a bank account for the benefit of another person but maintains control of the money until his death. Prior to your elder's death, he has the right to withdraw funds at any time. Your elder's beneficiary can't touch the money while your elder is still alive. This is also known as a revocable trust using a bank account. Only thirty-six states allow this type of trust, so check with your financial adviser or attorney to find out if this is even an option in your state. After your elder's death, the trust transfers to the beneficiary without a will or probate.

Even if this trust is available in your state, your elder may not want to go through the expense of setting it up. He can have the same control with a POD account and avoid the hassle and expense of establishing the trust.

Question 115: **What are TOD accounts?**

Transfer-on-death accounts operate in a similar fashion to POD accounts. The primary difference is that TOD accounts are used for publicly traded securities and debt obligations. While the registered owner is alive, she maintains total control over the securities in the account. After she dies, the securities transfer to the designated payee without a will or probate. The beneficiary designation is revocable, so the owner of the TOD can change the designee at any time while she is alive.

Question 116: **What are gifts causa mortis?**

In a few states, your elder can make a revocable gift called a gift causa mortis if your elder believes that he is near death. Death must be imminent for this will substitute to be used, but it can reduce gift taxes. *Causa mortis* is Latin for "contemplation of death." A gift causa mortis is both conditional and revocable. If your elder sets up this type of gift and survives the illness or other peril that he thought would result in his death, the gift is automatically revoked. Your elder can revoke the gift at any time for any reason if he is alive.

This type of will substitute is rarely used as an estate-planning tool. Most attorneys will recommend a trust or other formal arrangement if your elder wishes to designate a gift after his death.

Question 117: **What are revocable living trusts?**

All states recognize the use of revocable living trusts. With this type of trust, your elder transfers assets to someone but keeps the power to revoke the trust at any time. To avoid probate, your elder must fund this type of trust before he dies.

The trust agreement can be drawn up to transfer the assets to designated beneficiaries upon your elder's death, or your elder can designate a later time to transfer the assets to his beneficiaries. All assets in a revocable trust can be transferred to the designated beneficiaries without a will or probate, as long as your elder doesn't revoke the trust prior to his death.

Question 118: **What are irrevocable living trusts?**

An irrevocable living trust has almost all the same characteristics of a revocable living trust, discussed in Question 117. The primary difference is that the person who grants the trust to someone cannot change his mind later. The beneficiaries of the trust have a vested interest in the trust, and that interest cannot be revoked.

Question 119: **How can an elder use provisions in contracts to avoid a will?**

Every time an employee fills out a form for life insurance or an employer-sponsored retirement plan, he is signing a contract that likely has provisions to avoid the need for a will or probate. When a person designates a beneficiary as part of those forms, that person is essentially completing a will substitute. The assets in your elder's retirement account or the proceeds from the life insurance policy will transfer to his designated beneficiaries automatically without probate. Any life insurance policy, individual retirement account, annuity, or other type of contract your elder signs designating a beneficiary works the same way as employer plans after your elder's death.

Question 120: **What are the advantages of a will substitute?**

The biggest advantage of any will substitute is that it helps a person's heirs avoid the expensive costs and delays of having to go through probate. Using a will substitute, your elder can transfer his assets privately without having to file them with the probate court.

Many will substitutes are revocable, so your elder maintains control over the disposition of those assets while he is still alive. This also can be a disadvantage because revocable assets are used as part of the owner's gross estate and are taxable at death.

Question 121: **What are the disadvantages of a will substitute?**

The biggest disadvantage of a will substitute is that your elder must fund the substitute prior to his death—that is, your elder must put the assets intended for inclusion in the trust immediately. This can be a big factor if your elder is funding a trust, POD, or TOD. Will substitutes can be costly, especially if your elder wants to set up a revocable or irrevocable living trust. Your elder must hire an attorney to establish the trust, and your elder may need to pay maintenance fees as assets in the trust are purchased or sold. Your elder also will need to file tax returns if he sets up an irrevocable living trust.

Chapter **12**

DEALING WITH TAXES

WHEN YOU START helping your elder with her finances, you'll need to deal with several types of taxes. Initially, you'll have to worry about Social Security and income taxes, if your elder is still working. You'll also need to plan for the possibility of estate taxes.

Estate taxes, or "death taxes," as they are frequently called, are in a state of flux and will be until the U.S. Congress determines what it will do after 2010. In 2008, the first $2 million of an estate was excluded from taxes. In 2009, the exclusion amount will increase to $3.5 million. Then in 2010, the estate tax will be repealed—if your elder dies that year, your family won't have to pay estate taxes. But if Congress doesn't act to extend that repeal of the estate tax law, in 2011, estate taxes could go back to excluding just the first $1 million in assets. This chapter explains the law as it is currently written, but be aware that the law likely will change in 2011 or before then. This makes it difficult to do long-term estate planning.

Question 122: **How does preparing taxes differ once an elder starts to collect Social Security?**

Every year in retirement, your elder will have to determine whether she owes taxes on her Social Security benefits. When helping your elder with the taxes, you'll need to compare the base amount for her filing status to one-half of her Social Security benefits plus all her other income, including tax-exempt interest.

What is your elder's base amount? It depends on how she is filing. By IRS standards, your elder's base amount is:

- $25,000 if your elder is single, head of household, or a qualifying widow(er)
- $25,000 if your elder is married filing separately and lived apart from her spouse for the current tax year
- $32,000 if your elders are married and filing jointly
- $0 if your elders are married and filing separately and lived with each other at any time during the current tax year

If your elder's total income is more than her base amount, her benefits could be taxable. If your elder files a joint return, you must combine her income and benefits with her spouse's when doing this comparison. Even if your elder's spouse is not collecting benefits, you must add in his income when trying to determine whether your elder's benefits are taxable.

If the only income your elder receives is from Social Security, her benefits most likely are not taxable. Your elder may not even have to file a tax return. If your elder does have income in addition to her benefits, you may be stuck filing a return even if none of her benefits is taxable. If the total of one-half of your elder's benefits plus all other income is more than $34,000 (if your elder is single) or $44,000 (if your elders are filing jointly), then your elder likely will have to pay income taxes on part of her Social Security benefit. For most, the amount of taxable income is 50 percent of benefits for some high earners, but as much as 85 percent of benefits can be taxable. This does not mean that your elder pays taxes at an 85 percent tax rate. What it means is that 85 percent of your elder's benefits are taxable at the current income tax rate.

Question 123: **Can an elder earn money and collect Social Security?**

Your elder can earn money and collect Social Security, but if she hasn't reached her full retirement age, she may lose benefits. In my answer to Question 124, I'll talk more about the rules for going back to work. Question 122 addresses the possibility of Social Security income's being taxed if your elder earns too much.

Question 124: **What happens to earnings if an elder works before reaching full retirement age according to the rules of Social Security?**

Your elder doesn't have to worry about any earnings rules as long as she has reached her full retirement age. That age used to be sixty-five, but it is gradually increasing to sixty-seven. Most baby boomers reach full retirement age at sixty-six. If your elder retired early, she could lose some benefits until she reaches full retirement age.

The Social Security Administration considers two levels of exemptions for earnings:

- There is a lower earnings threshold for people between age sixty-two and their full retirement age. The Social Security Administration withholds $1 of benefits for every $2 of earnings in excess of the lower threshold for younger retirees.
- There is a higher earnings threshold for people in the year they will reach their full retirement age. In the year of attaining their full retirement age, retirees are allowed a higher threshold of earnings, and only $1 of every $3 will be withheld.

In 2008, the higher threshold of exempt earnings between the age of sixty-two and full retirement age was $36,120. The lower threshold was $13,560, which is adjusted by a formula based on the national wage index each year.

Question 125: **What is the retirement earnings test (RET)?**

The retirement earnings test is the method used to manage the principle that "one must be retired in order to collect retirement benefits from Social Security's old-age insurance program." That statement was in the original law. The RET took many forms over the years, but its primary purpose was to reduce benefits if a retiree started working again.

Today, the rules have changed to allow a retiree to work as much as she wants once she has reached full retirement age without any reduction in benefits. Your elder has to worry about the RET only if she retires early and wants to go back to work. In my answer to Question 124, I talk about the rules for working after an early retirement.

Question 126: **How much can an elder lose in earnings if she fails the RET?**

How much your elder can lose in earnings if she fails the RET depends on her age and when she reaches full retirement age. Full retirement age used to be sixty-five for everyone. Today, that age is gradually increasing to sixty-seven. Anyone born after 1960 will have to wait until age sixty-seven for full retirement. People born during the baby boom will have to wait until age sixty-six.

If your elder goes back to work before reaching full retirement age, she can lose as much as $1 benefit for every $2 earned over the allowable limit. The allowable limit for most early retirees is $13,560. If your elder is within twelve months of her full retirement age, she loses only $1 for every $30 of benefits. She also can earn up to $36,120 in this last year before full retirement age.

Question 127: **What income must be considered when determining whether an elder must pay taxes on her Social Security benefits?**

Income that is taxed during retirement is not that different from the income your elder received prior to retiring. Taxable income can include compensation for services, interest, dividends, rents, royalties, income from partnerships, estate and trust income, gains from sales or exchanges of property, and business income of all kinds.

Any wages or other compensation your elder receives for services is treated as income in the same way as before your elder retired. Your elder does not need to report any income amounts for supportive services or out-of-pocket expense reimbursements if your elder is involved in certain volunteer programs, including the Retired Senior Volunteer Program (RSVP), Foster Grandparent Program, Senior Companion Program, and Service Corps of Retired Executives (SCORE).

In addition to the traditional sources of income a worker receives, your elder also may get retirement plan distributions, purchased annuities, railroad benefits, or military benefits.

Question 128: **How much tax could an elder have to pay on her Social Security benefits?**

The tax your elder will have to pay on her Social Security benefits is based on the earnings test discussed in Question 125. Remember that the amount of tax will depend on your elder's tax bracket. Even if her Social Security benefits are taxable, they will be taxed at their current income tax rate, which can be no higher than 35 percent.

Question 129: **Does an elder have to pay taxes on pensions?**

Your elder will have to pay taxes on most types of pensions. Some disability pensions are not taxable.

Question 130: **Does an elder have to pay taxes on withdrawals from her retirement savings?**

Your elder will have to pay taxes at her current income tax rate on withdrawals from most types of retirement savings. The only type of retirement savings that is not taxable is the Roth IRA.

Question 131: **How do Roth IRAs differ from traditional IRAs when it comes to taxes?**

A traditional IRA grows tax deferred, but all money taken out of the IRA at retirement is subject to tax at a person's current income tax rate. Roth IRAs grow tax free and can be taken out tax free as long as your elder is at least age 59½. There are some exceptions to the Roth IRA that allow for early withdrawals without penalty. But if your elder takes out any of the gains that your elder made on a Roth IRA before reaching age 59½, those gains will be taxed at current interest rates with a few exceptions that I won't go into here since this is an eldercare book.

Question 132: **Will an elder have to worry about estimated taxes?**

Your elder may have to worry about estimated taxes. There are two possible situations in which your elder may have to pay estimated taxes:

1. She goes back to work and earns enough money that her Social Security benefits become taxable (see Question 122).

2. Your elder's retirement earnings exceed $34,000 (if single) and $44,000 (if married filing jointly). It's possible that your elder will have to pay taxes on her Social Security income, so she may need to pay estimated taxes.

If you think that for any reason your elder's Social Security benefits will be taxed or if your elder gets retirement pensions for which taxes are not withheld, your may need to recommend to your elder that she pay estimated tax. Also, if your elder has a lot of investment income, estimated taxes could become a necessity. Essentially, the rules for estimated taxes are no different for someone who is collecting Social Security than they are for someone who is not collecting Social Security.

Question 133: **What is the federal unified transfer tax system?**

The federal unified transfer tax system combined the gift taxes (taxes on gifts made during one's lifetime) and estate taxes (taxes on one's assets passed on at one's death) in 1976. Prior to that time, the two types of taxes were separate. Today, the same tax rates are used to determine both one's estate and gift tax liability. With this system, a $250,000 taxable gift would be taxed in the same way as a $250,000 taxable estate, provided that there had not been taxable transfers prior to one's death. The maximum gift or estate tax rate for 2007 to 2009 is 45 percent for gifts or estate exceeding the maximum exclusions.

With the passage of the Economic Growth and Tax Relief Reconciliation Act of 2001, the gift tax maximum exclusion from taxation is $1 million, and the maximum exclusion for estate taxes is $2 million. Anything one leaves to one's spouse is entirely excluded from gift or estate taxes, provided one's spouse is a U.S. citizen.

This tax system also makes it possible for your elder to transfer her assets by a lifetime gift or a bequest at death to a qualified charity and reduce the tax liability of the estate. The amount of your elder's estate is cumulative, and both gifts and transfers of property after your elder's death are totaled to calculate the full value of your elder's estate under the unified system.

Question 134: **What is a gift tax?**

A gift tax is a tax due on gifts of more than $1 million during your elder's lifetime. Your elder can avoid ever having to pay a gift tax by giving $12,000 or less to an individual each year. A couple can give up to $24,000 because the law treats the gift as though one-half of the gift were given by each spouse. These limits can be adjusted by the government annually for inflation. Provided that your elder doesn't give more than $12,000 in any one year, all the gifts could be given without using up any of her $1 million gift tax exclusion.

Your elder also can give away an unlimited amount of money provided that the gift goes directly to an educational institution for tuition. Your elder can pay tuition for each of her grandchildren without having to worry about gift taxes. Your elder also can avoid gift taxes if she pays a medical provider for any uninsured medical expenses for a third party. For example, suppose wealthy grandparents want to fund cancer treatments for a grandchild, and the amount will exceed $12,000. As long as they pay the cancer treatment center directly, the money given will not be included in gift tax calculations.

Question 135: **What is an estate tax?**

An estate tax is a tax on one's estate after one's death. When a person dies, any property or assets that are left behind become part of that estate. The federal government taxes that estate before the assets can be transferred to one's heirs. The amount of tax depends on the size of the estate and when one dies. In 2007 and 2008, the first $2 million of an estate was excluded from taxes. In 2009, the exclusion amount increases to $3.5 million. Then in 2010, no estate taxes will be due. In 2011, if Congress doesn't act fast, estate taxes will be due on any estate worth more than $1 million. Tax rates would range from 41 percent on estates worth more than $1 million to as high as 60 percent on estates between $10 million and $17,184,000. Estates worth more than $17,184,000 would be taxed at a rate of 55 percent.

Question 136: **What is a generation-skipping tax?**

The federal government doesn't want to miss collecting taxes during each generation, so if your elder tries to avoid taxes by giving her estate to her grandchildren rather than to you, she might have to pay a generation-skipping tax. For example, suppose your elder decides to give a sizable gift of $1 million to your child. Your elder would have to pay both the gift taxes and the generation-skipping taxes on that gift. Your elder can avoid paying any gift taxes by applying that gift to your applicable credit amount of $1 million in gift taxes. Your elder can still skip generations by giving money to her grandchildren or great-grandchildren or to anyone else who is more than one generation younger than she is, because a gift tax is applied only once, even if more than one generation is skipped with the gift. Your elder won't be subject to generation-skipping taxes if she pays medical or educational expenses directly for any person who is more than one generation younger than she is.

Question 137: **What is EGTRRA, and how does it affect the federal unified transfer tax system?**

The Economic Growth and Tax Relief Reconciliation Act of 2001 (EGTRRA) created a temporary change to the gift and estate tax system that expires in 2011. Congress wanted to keep the tax cut to a certain size, and repealing the gift and estate tax completely would have been too expensive. So instead, they passed this nightmare that leaves everyone guessing as to what will happen to gift and estate taxes in the future. It's very hard to plan an estate when you have no idea what the tax will be on that estate in 2011. If Congress does not act, then the estate and gift taxes will revert to what they were before the passage of EGTRRA, which means just $1 million will be excluded from gift and estate taxes. Tax rates would range from 41 percent on estates worth more than $1 million to as high as 60 percent on estates between $10 million and $17,184,000. Estates worth more than $17,184,000 would be taxed at a rate of 55 percent.

Question 138: **What is the marital deduction?**

If your elder is married, the marital deduction allows her to offset or reduce her estate's tax liability by transferring it to her spouse. Your elder also gets a gift tax marital deduction to offset any gift tax liability when she gives her spouse a gift. Essentially, anything one gives as a gift to a spouse or leaves to a spouse in one's estate will not be taxed thanks to the marital deduction.

Question 139: **What is the charitable deduction?**

Your elder can reduce her tax liability with a gift to a charitable institution using the charitable deduction. Any gift or bequest to a charitable institution will reduce the taxable amount of your elder's estate. For example, suppose your elder dies in 2009 with an estate worth $4 million. In 2009, $3.5 million will be excluded from estate taxes. Your elder can avoid estate taxes completely by donating $500,000 to charity. (See Chapter 14 for how to use charitable donations in estate planning.)

Question 140: **What is the applicable credit (or unified credit)?**

The applicable credit (formerly known as the unified credit) allows a person to exclude a certain amount of her taxable transfer from the calculation of estate tax. This credit is part of the Internal Revenue tax code. Congress periodically determines the amount of a person's estate that will be free from taxes.

Question 141: **What is the fair market value of an estate?**

Figuring out how much one's estate is worth depends on the value established for the assets one is transferring either as a gift or after one's death. The U.S. Department of the Treasury defines fair market value (FMV) as "the price at which property would change hands between a willing buyer and a willing seller, neither being under any compulsion to buy or sell and both having reasonable knowledge of relevant facts. The fair market value of a particular item of property includible in the decedent's gross estate is not to be determined by a forced sale price. Nor is the fair market value of an item of property to be determined by the sale price of the item in a market other than that in which such item is most commonly sold to the public, taking into account the location of the item wherever appropriate."

The IRS will question certain types of property transfer. For example, the price an employee pays for property from an employer could be questioned. If your elder plans to sell her business to an employee to avoid estate taxes, expect some scrutiny from the IRS regarding its value. Also, a forced-sale situation, such as an auction, cannot be used to determine the fair market value. The price the IRS will use to determine value is the retail value of the property.

Question 142: **What date is used for the valuation of property?**

When an executor is determining the value of property in the estate, he has two possible dates from which to choose. The value of the property in the estate can be based on the value at the time of your elder's death, or it can be valued six months after your elder's death.

In either case, the executor must value all property in the estate based on one of these two dates. For example, suppose the value of a stock portfolio dropped rapidly during the six months after your elder's death. It may make sense to use the value date six months after the death to save taxes on the estate. But if during that same time other assets, such as real estate, rose dramatically in price, then the executor would need to calculate the estate based on both dates to determine which date would result in the lowest tax liability. The executor must use the same date for valuing all the property. He can't choose one date for some of the property and the other date for the rest of the property.

Question 143: **How does a person report and pay federal estate tax?**

Whether you have to file an estate tax return upon your elder's death will depend on the value of the estate. If the value of the estate does not exceed the maximum applicable exclusion amount, which is $2 million in 2007 and 2008 and $3.5 million in 2009, then no tax return must be filed. In 2010, when the estate tax is fully repealed, no one who inherits an estate from someone who dies that year will have to file an estate tax return. But in 2011, unless the law is changed, you will need to file an estate tax return for any estate worth more than $1 million.

In many cases, the executor or executrix is responsible for filing the tax returns. If all assets were transferred using will substitutes (see Chapter 11), the recipients of the assets will be responsible for filing the tax return.

If you must file an estate tax return, it is due nine months after your elder's death, but often the full value of the estate is not known at that time. Sometimes it takes longer to determine the value of certain assets, such as those of a small-business owner. If more than nine months are needed, you can file for an automatic extension of six months by filling out IRS Form 4768. To receive further extensions, you will need to explain why you can't complete the forms.

Chapter 13

CALCULATING THE ESTATE TAX

CALCULATING ESTATE TAX can be a mathematical nightmare. This chapter reviews the basics of what you must consider to calculate your elder's estate tax after his death.

Question 144: **What are the key parts of calculating estate tax?**

The calculation of the tax is simple once you find the value of the net estate. Getting to that value is where the complications arise. Once you know the true value of the estate assets (discussed in greater detail in questions 141 and 142), here is the actual formula for finding the net estate tax due:

- Take the gross estate value, and subtract the amount allowed by deductions (see questions 138 to 140 and 155 to 162). This gives the taxable estate.
- Now add taxable lifetime transfers since 1976 (see Chapter 12). This gives your tax base.
- Next, multiply the tax base by the applicable estate tax rate. This gives the tentative estate tax (see Question 165).

- Finally, subtract any credits to find your net estate tax due (see Chapter 12 and questions 164 to 168).

In the following questions, I'll break down the key parts of this calculation and discuss how the estate tax calculation differs from the income tax calculation.

Question 145: **What is the difference in calculating estate tax versus income tax?**

The primary difference between income tax and estate tax calculations is how one determines the applicable tax rate (see Chapter 12). For income tax, you calculate your taxes based on the level of income earned in a given year. For estate tax, you need to calculate what remains in an estate as of the date of your elder's death. You also need to add all cumulative taxable transfers of wealth since 1976, when the gift tax and estate tax were combined. That means any taxable gifts given to family over the years must be included as part of the total estate.

If your elder's estate involves more than the current maximum allowed to be excluded from tax—$2 million in 2007 and 2008 and $3.5 million in 2009—you must be able to calculate how much was given in taxable gifts over the years as well as how much is left in the estate. Taxable gifts are gifts of more than $12,000 in any one year ($24,000 for a couple). The government can adjust this amount annually for inflation. If taxes were already paid on these gifts, they can be subtracted as credits, so the estate is not taxed twice. You will face a big problem if your elder has not kept proper records and you can't perform this calculation.

Question 146: **What is the gross estate?**

The gross estate serves as the starting point for all estate tax calculations. Although in many states the gross estate is the same as the probate estate, this is not true at the federal level. In addition to the probate estate, you must add any items not included in probate, such as property transferred by will substitutes (see Chapter 11), insurance proceeds, and retirement benefits.

Question 147: **Which property is calculated in the gross estate?**

When trying to determine which property should be included in the gross estate, the key question to ask is whether your elder was in possession of that property at death—no matter what kind of property is involved. The gross estate can include antiques, art, bank accounts, bonds, cars, certificates of deposit, contracts, houses, leases, life insurance policies on the lives of others, partnership interests, promissory notes, royalties, and stocks. All of these assets must be included in the calculation of the gross estate. Even if your elder had only a partial interest in any of these items, value for these items must be included in the gross estate. For example, if your elder owned community property with his spouse, then one-half the value of that property must be included in the gross estate.

In addition, income that is not includable in your elder's income tax returns for the year of his death must be calculated and included in the gross estate. This income is called income in respect of decedent (IRD) and includes bonuses, deferred compensation, expense reimbursements, interest accrued and payable to your elder in the future, proceeds from installment sales, renewal commissions, and any other type of income that will be received by the estate in the future.

Question 148: **Is life insurance part of the gross estate?**

The insurance proceeds from any insurance policy owned by your elder at death must be included in the gross estate. Even if your elder does not own the life insurance policy outright (as might be the case with a policy owned by an employer), if your elder had some incident of ownership, such as the right to name a beneficiary, then the proceeds must be included in the gross estate. Examples of incident of ownership include the right to borrow against the policy cash values; the right to cash in, surrender, or cancel the policy; the right to pledge the policy as collateral for a loan; and the right to receive policy dividends.

Your elder can avoid including insurance proceeds from a life insurance policy by assigning all incidents of ownership to an irrevocable life insurance trust. But your elder must set up this trust at least three years before his death in order for the proceeds to be left out of the estate.

Question 149: **How is joint property calculated in the gross estate?**

How joint property is calculated depends upon the type of joint ownership. Two types of ownership do not include the right of survivorship: tenancy in common and traditional community property. In these situations, your elder is considered to have a fractional interest in the property, and that fractional interest is included in the gross estate.

If the ownership includes a right of survivorship, such as joint tenancy with right of survival or tenancy by the entirety, then the portion of the property included in the gross estate will depend on the relationship of the owners. If the joint owners are husband and wife, one-half of the value of the property is included in the gross estate no matter how much each spouse contributed to the property. There is an exception to this if the joint tenancy was created before 1977. In that case, the surviving spouse can choose to use the rules for joint owners who are not spouses.

For joint owners who are not spouses, the portion of the property's value that will be included in your elder's estate after death will depend on your elder's contribution when the property was purchased. For example, if you can prove that your elder contributed only 33 percent of the cost to purchase that joint property, then only 33 percent of the current value of the property would be included in your elder's gross estate.

Question 150: **Are survivorship benefits (retirement benefits, pensions, annuities) included in the gross estate?**

Inclusion of survivorship benefits for retirement benefits, pensions, or annuities in the gross estate depends on what happens to the value of those benefits upon your elder's death. In some cases, the benefits for an annuity may end, and nothing will be added to your elder's gross estate. If the benefits will be paid in a lump sum upon death, then the lump sum is added to the gross estate.

If the periodic benefits will continue to be paid after your elder's death, then you must calculate the present value of those benefits. That present value should be added to the gross estate.

Formulas for calculating present value depend upon the type of annuity. If the annuity is a private annuity (any annuity issued by an entity other than an insurance company, such as an employer), use the interest set by the IRS, called the applicable federal rate, to calculate the present value. The IRS publishes valuation tables to make this calculation easier.

If the annuity is provided by a commercial insurance company, the present value is measured by the premium charged for a newly issued single life annuity on the survivor's life, which is the amount one would have to pay to buy the same type of annuity on the survivor's life.

Question 151: **What are lifetime transfers, and how are they included in the gross estate?**

Even if your elder gives away large portions of his estate prior to death, those portions still must be included when calculating the gross estate. Each year, your elder can give a gift of up to $12,000 to any person without having to worry about its being a taxable transfer for gift or estate tax purposes. A couple can give up to $24,000 to any individual. Remember that the government can adjust the annual exclusion amount for inflation.

Larger gifts are considered lifetime transfers and are taxable through gift taxes or estate taxes. Up to $1 million of taxable lifetime transfers are excluded from the gift tax, but any gifts above that level are taxed. When calculating the gross estate, all taxable lifetime transfers must be added to the calculation.

Question 152: **If a person retains a lifetime interest in property, is that included in the gross estate?**

If your elder transfers his property to a family member prior to his death but retains an interest in that property until his death, then the value of that property must be included in his gross estate. For example, suppose your elder gives his home to your brother or sister but keeps a life estate in the property (that is, he continues to control the property until his death). The value of the property will be included as part of his gross estate.

This is also true if he establishes an irrevocable trust but keeps the right to receive income from that trust while he is alive. He can stipulate that the recipient of the property will receive income from that trust for fifteen years, and as long as he dies after the last payment, the value of the trust will not be included in his gross estate. But if he stipulates that the payments from the trust will continue until one month prior to his death, the trust value must be included in his gross estate. In fact, any measurement of your elder's ownership in property that is based on his death will make that property subject to estate taxes.

Question 153: **What is the three-year inclusionary rule?**

Even if your elder gives property away, if that gift of property was within three years of his death, it still may need to be included in his gross estate. This is known as the three-year inclusionary rule, which is sometimes referred to as the "transfers in contemplation of death" rule. There are three basic parts to this rule:

1. **Transferring retained interest in a property within three years of one's death**—If your elder gives up his rights to a life estate within three years of his death, the value of that property still will be included in your elder's gross estate.
2. **Transfers of insurance**—If your elder transfers all incidents of ownership in a life insurance policy on his life to someone else within three years of his death, then the proceeds of the life insurance policy must be included in your elder's gross estate.
3. **Gift taxes**—If your elder pays gift taxes on any gifts within three years of his death, these taxes are included in the gross estate.

Question 154: **What can be deducted from the gross estate?**

Your elder's gross estate can be reduced with many different kinds of deductions. Common deductions include:

- Debts
- Funeral expenses
- Administrative expenses
- Casualty and theft losses
- State estate taxes paid
- Marital deduction
- Charitable deductions

After the first four deductions are subtracted, this is known as the adjusted gross estate. When the last three deductions are taken, this becomes the taxable estate. (More about what can be included in these deductions is discussed in questions 155 through 162.)

Question 155: **How are debts, mortgages, and liens deducted from the gross estate?**

Any financial obligations owed by your elder can be deducted from the gross estate. This includes accrued rent and lease payments, credit card balances, open accounts at retailers, mortgages, promissory notes, and property liens, as well as any due but unpaid taxes.

Question 156: **How does a person calculate funeral expenses to be deducted from the gross estate?**

As long as the funeral expenses are reasonable, they can be deducted from the estate, even if you pay cash out of your pocket and then deduct the expenses from the estate. Reasonable expenses can include a headstone, even if it is somewhat extravagant; a burial plot and its future care; travel expenses of people necessary for the ceremony; and the costs of a meal for guests after the ceremony.

Question 157: **What administrative expenses can be deducted from the gross estate?**

The cost of managing your elder's estate can be high, and any reasonable expenses can be deducted from the gross estate. These can include the appraisal fees, attorneys' fees, insurance bills to protect the property until sold or distributed to heirs, personal representative's commission, probate fees, rent (for example, to keep a retail establishment open until a business is sold or distributed to heirs), safekeeping fees (for example, to pay security for the property or maintenance on the property if needed), trust fees, and utility bills.

The federal estate tax return is due nine months after your elder's death. If the estate remains open and undistributed at that time, you can ask for a six-month extension or estimate what all the administrative expenses will be. You also can decide to claim any unclaimed administrative expenses on the final estate federal income tax return.

Question 158: **Can a person deduct estate taxes paid to a foreign government?**

If your elder owned property in another country, his estate may be subject to estate taxes by that foreign government. The U.S. government permits you to deduct these taxes from your elder's estate provided that the property located in that foreign country is included in calculation of the gross estate in the United States or the property was transferred for public, charitable, or religious uses. Although this deduction is available, few people use it. Instead, they use a tax credit that is available in the credit section of the taxable estate calculation, which usually saves more money.

Question 159: **What theft and casualty losses can be deducted from the gross estate?**

You can deduct any theft or casualty losses that are not covered by insurance and that are incurred after your elder's death and before the distribution to beneficiaries or heirs. For example, if your elder's house burns down before the estate is settled and the insurance on the home covers only 90 percent of the fair market value, the portion of the value not covered by the insurance company can be deducted from the gross estate.

Question 160: **What state estate taxes can be deducted from the gross estate?**

When the Economic Growth and Tax Relief Reconciliation Act of 2001 was passed, the credit for state estate taxes was killed, and a deduction was added instead. A deduction is worth less than a credit; although a deduction reduces the amount of the gross estate, a credit reduces the amount of the taxes due.

Through 2009, you can deduct state estates taxes. If your elder dies in 2010, there will be no federal estate taxes, so this deduction won't matter. If your elder dies after 2010 and there is no change to the law, then the old estate tax law will become law again, and the state estate tax credit can be used.

Question 161: **What is the marital deduction, and how is it calculated?**

If your elder gives his entire estate—even if it's worth $100 million—to his surviving spouse, the marital deduction can erase the potential estate tax liability to zero, as long as the money transfers to your elder's spouse in a qualified way. The best way for your elder to guarantee this deduction is to pass property to his spouse through a will, beneficiary designation, or right of survivorship. This removes any chance of doubt that the property was passed in a qualified way.

If your elder dies without a will and his spouse receives property under state intestacy law, doubts could arise. In most cases, your elder's spouse would still be able to take the marital deduction—but why risk it? It's best to ensure that all property transfers the way your elder wants it to transfer by drawing up a will, beneficiary designation, or survivorship.

Note that the marital deduction can be applied only to a marriage between one man and one woman. Marriages between same-sex couples are not recognized in federal law after the passage of the Defense of Marriage Act.

Question 162: **How much in charitable contributions can be deducted from the gross estate?**

The amount your elder can deduct for a charitable contribution is unlimited, provided that the charity qualifies under federal estate tax law. If the charity is a public charity, there is little doubt about qualification, because whether the charity qualifies for tax deductibility is publicly known. Your elder may find it more difficult to prove qualification if the charity is a private foundation. The IRS publishes a list of charities that qualify for gift and estate tax purposes. If your elder wants to make a charitable contribution in his will, contact the IRS before writing that will to ensure that the charity qualifies for federal estate tax deductions.

The law allows this deduction for the contribution of cash or property only. Your elder could not secure a deduction by giving a charity the right to use his property for free; he would have to give the charity title to the property.

Question 163: **What are adjusted taxable gifts, and how do they affect the calculation of the estate tax?**

All post-1976 gifts made by your elder must be adjusted to remove the taxable portion of the gifts. This is done by including gift items based on their value at the time of the gift, while other items in the gross estate are valued at fair market value at your elder's death or six months after the death if that time frame is chosen. This can make a significant difference in the total of the gross estate, especially if the gift changed in value between the time it was given and the time of your elder's death. For example, suppose your elder gave his home to you or one of your siblings and moved to a smaller place. At the time of the gift, the home was worth $150,000, but at the time of your elder's death, the home was worth $300,000. Only the $150,000 would need to be included when calculating the gross estate and the gift or estate taxes. Any gift taxes paid on the gift are subtracted as a credit, so taxes won't be paid twice.

Question 164: **What is the gift taxes payable credit?**

Any gift taxes paid out of pocket for gifts given after 1976 can be subtracted from the gross estate tax. This gift taxes payable credit can be taken only if your elder made taxable transfers of property during his lifetime that cumulatively exceeded the gift tax applicable exclusion amount in any one year. The exclusion amount in a year is $12,000 for an individual and $24,000 for a couple. The annual exclusion amount can be adjusted annually for inflation.

Question 165: **What is the applicable credit?**

The applicable credit is the full amount of the estate tax credit allowed in the year of the decedent's death. One is entitled to the full credit because all gifts have been included in the gross amount of the estate. The following IRS charts show the 2007 federal tax rates for estates and trusts and the tax-applicable exclusion amount.

2007 Federal Estate and Trust Tax Rates

If taxable income is:	The tax is:
Not over $2,150	15% of the taxable income
Over $2,150 but not over $5,000	$322.50 plus 25% of the excess over $2,150
Over $5,000 but not over $7,650	$1,035 plus 28% of the excess over $5,000
Over $7,650 but not over $10,450	$1,777 plus 33% of the excess over $7,650
Over $10,450	$2,701 plus 35% of the excess over $10,450

An estate tax return for a U.S. citizen or resident needs to be filed only if the gross estate exceeds the applicable exclusion amount, listed here:

Increased Estate Tax Applicable Exclusion Amount
Applicable Exclusion Amounts

Year	Exclusion Amount
2006, 2007, and 2008	$2,000,000
2009	$3,500,000
2010	No Estate Tax

Question 166: **What is the credit for federal gift taxes?**

This credit is allowed for any gift taxes paid out of pocket prior to 1977. The credit also can be taken for gift taxes paid out of pocket by your elder's spouse on gifts for which your elder was the donor but the gifts were split. The credit that can be taken is equal to the lesser of the gift tax or the estate tax paid on the property in question. The purpose of this credit is to avoid double taxation of transferred property.

Question 167: **What is the credit for foreign estate taxes?**

This credit is allowed if your elder paid taxes on property to a foreign country, as long as the property is included in the gross estate in the United States. The credit is limited to the lesser of the foreign estate or the amount of the U.S. estate attributable to the property in question.

Question 168: **What is the prior transfer credit?**

To avoid double taxation, this credit is allowed on taxes paid for property received ten years before or two years after the death of your elder. If the property was included in the taxable estate of the transferor and a beneficial interest in the property was transferred to your elder, the elder's estate does not need to include any interest in the property at death. This credit can be used even if your elder sold the property or gave it to charity.

Chapter 14

ESTATE TAX PLANNING WITH YOUR ELDER

CHAPTER 13 PRESENTED the key factors that go into calculating gift and estate taxes. This chapter focuses on minimizing the taxes that will need to be paid on your elder's estate. Through various types of trusts, your elder can significantly reduce his estate taxes.

Question 169: **What are the goals of estate tax planning?**

There are three important reasons to do estate tax planning:

1. To lower the value of your elder's gross estate
2. To increase the deductions your elder's estate will be eligible for or entitled to take
3. To maintain the estate's eligibility for as many credits as possible

These may sound obvious, but they're not always easy to attain. Consult an estate tax planner to ensure that the strategies your elder plans to use will actually work when the taxes are calculated on his estate.

Question 170: **How can an elder reduce the gross estate?**

Your elder can reduce his gross estate by giving away assets during his lifetime. However, to avoid ending up with the full value of these assets included in his estate, he must give them away more than three years before his death. Otherwise, the three-year inclusionary rule (see Question 153) could force those assets to be included in your elder's gross estate. For this strategy to work, your elder also must give the property away without retaining any rights.

Although your elder must include the value of gifts in his gross estate, a gift of property more than three years before his death is included based on the value of that gift at the time it was given rather than at the time of your elder's death. For example, suppose your father gave you and your sister title to property worth $100,000 in 2000. By the time of his death, that property had jumped in value to $300,000. When calculating the estate, the property value would be $100,000, not $300,000. Had your father held on to that property, the gross estate would have to include the higher $300,000 value.

Question 171: **How can an elder preserve or increase the estate tax deductions and credits?**

There are three tools that can help your elder preserve or increase his estate tax deduction and credits. They are as follows:

1. **Marital deduction**—This deduction is unlimited for any property left to your elder's spouse. Any assets given to the spouse can delay taxation until after the death of the surviving spouse.
2. **Charitable deduction**—The deduction is unlimited for any property left to a qualified charity. The IRS publishes a list of qualified charities for federal estate tax purposes. Make sure that the charity your elder picks is on that list.
3. **Applicable credit amount**—Your elder can end up giving too much of his estate to his spouse or a charity without taking full advantage of the applicable credit amount.

In planning your elder's estate, make sure that he considers the applicable credit amount before increasing his deductions with marital or charitable deductions. Otherwise, your elder can end up writing off all taxes when the first spouse dies and paying even more taxes on the total estate when the surviving spouse dies because the marginal tax rate is higher.

Question 172: **How does an elder manage the marital deduction for estate tax planning purposes?**

There are no taxes on gifts between spouses, so when working with your elder to plan his estate, you can use the marital deduction to minimize taxes. The IRS allows transfers between husband and wife because it sees a couple as one economic entity rather than two.

The use of a marital deduction does not eliminate the payment of estate taxes, however. It just delays payment until after the second spouse's death.

Trusts generally cannot be used to minimize future taxes that must be paid on the marital estate when the second spouse dies, even though the marital deduction can delay those taxes. When managing the assets used as part of a marital deduction, trusts are often used for nontax reasons, including the following:

- Some trusts give the spouse who grants the trust control over who will get the assets after the spouse who receives the trust dies. For example, suppose your father wants to give his second wife a trust that she can use while she is alive but wants to give children from his first marriage rights to the remaining funds in the trust. He could accomplish this through a qualified terminable property (QTIP) trust. (I'll talk more about the QTIP trust in my answer to Question 175 and the bypass trust, another way of handling such situations, in Question 176.)
- If set up properly, a trust can protect assets from the claims of the beneficiaries' creditors.

- Trusts provide for professional management of assets, which might offer more expertise than the individual beneficiary may have.

Question 173: **What is the power of appointment trust (marital trust)?**

This is a common type of marital trust in which the recipient spouse gets an income interest for life and the power to decide where the remaining funds should go either during her lifetime or after her death. If the trust is given as a gift during her lifetime, then gift taxes apply. Any money left in the trust at the recipient spouse's death would be subject to estate tax. This type of marital trust is used if the spouse establishing the trust:

- Desires to leave the funds in trust rather than as an outright transfer of assets (In this case, a professional would manage the assets of the trust.)
- Decides to use the marital deduction for these assets
- Wants to give his spouse the maximum possible control over the assets
- Does not care if the recipient spouse changes the person who will receive any remaining funds after the death of the recipient spouse

Question 174: **What is an estate trust?**

In this trust, the spouse who establishes the trust names his surviving spouse as the sole beneficiary of the trust. Any income or money left in the trust at the end of the recipient spouse's lifetime would be distributed based on the provisions of the recipient spouse's will. The primary difference between this type of trust and a power of appointment trust is that income paid to the recipient spouse is discretionary and not mandatory. The trustee makes a determination about when to pay the recipient spouse income and how much that income should be.

The biggest advantage is that this trust qualifies for the marital deduction but doesn't make it mandatory to pay the recipient spouse anything. If a couple wants to get full advantage of the marital deduction yet leave all the money in the trust for their children, this is one possible vehicle to make that happen. Through her will, the recipient spouse maintains full control over who receives the money upon her death.

Question 175: **What is the QTIP trust?**

The qualified terminable property trust is similar to the power of appointment trust in how income is paid to the recipient spouse, but its key difference is that the spouse establishing the trust decides who will get any trust funds remaining after the death of the recipient spouse. The spouse establishing the trust maintains more control of the money than he would with a power of appointment trust. This trust qualifies for the marital deduction but leaves the distribution of assets to the discretion of the personal representative, who can decide to use the marital deduction for part or all of the trust assets. Use this trust if your elder wants:

- To leave property in trust rather than as an outright transfer
- To enable flexibility about whether the marital deduction should be used for the trust funds
- To ensure that his spouse will receive mandatory income for the rest of her life
- To name the recipient of any remaining funds in the trust after the death of the surviving spouse

Question 176: **What is bypass planning?**

To ensure that the appropriate amount of the estate does not fall under a marital or charitable deduction, which would use up a portion of the estate tax exclusion, your elder can use a bypass trust. This type of trust will not qualify for the marital deduction, because it will name the surviving spouse as just one of several income beneficiaries of the trust. As indicated earlier, it's important not to waste the estate tax applicable exclusion, because then all the assets that go to the surviving spouse become taxable. By adding both the husband's and wife's shares and putting all the assets in one pot at the death of the first spouse, the tax margin could be a lot higher when the surviving spouse dies. Your elder should use a bypass trust if he:

- Wants to leave property in trust rather than as an outright transfer
- Does not want to use the marital deduction for the assets placed in the trust
- Wants to include more than just his spouse as income beneficiaries
- Wants to control who will get the assets at the death of his spouse

Question 177: **What strategies can be used to combine marital and bypass trusts?**

If your elder knows that he will have to pay estate taxes, one of the best ways to minimize or delay those taxes is a combination of both marital and bypass trusts. Use the bypass trust to use up your elder's estate tax applicable exclusion, and then put the remaining assets in a marital trust, such as the power of appointment trust, to protect the rest of his assets from immediate estate taxes. Since this trust qualifies for the marital deduction, all assets in that trust will not be taxed until the death of the surviving spouse.

If your elder wants his surviving spouse to have less control of the assets and not argue about who should get those assets after his death, then use the QTIP trust rather than the power of appointment trust. Often a combination of the three trusts will be used, which will allow the surviving spouse full control of the power of appointment trust but leave the disbursement of the assets in the QTIP trust to the trustee so that money will be there for the children and grandchildren.

Question 178: **How does an elder use the charitable deduction in estate tax planning?**

The simplest way is to transfer the assets completely through a fee simple title to the cash or property your elder wants to leave to the charity. But often a person wants to leave only a partial interest in those assets. To make a partial charitable contribution that will meet the requirements of the charitable deduction, there are several types of trusts your elder can use, including the remainder trust, the charitable lead trust, and the charitable remainder annuity trust. (See questions 179 through 182 for a review of these types of trusts.) All these types of trusts guarantee that the charity will get some part of the property in the trust for which the deduction is allowed.

Question 179: **What is the remainder trust in a farm or personal residence?**

Your elder should use a remainder trust if he wants to make provisions for his farm or personal residence to be donated to a charity but guarantee that his surviving spouse can live on the farm or in the residence for the remainder of her life. The value of this property would then qualify for the charitable deduction.

If the person named to have the life estate is your elder's spouse, the marital deduction initially would be used to avoid estate taxes upon your elder's death. Upon the death of the surviving spouse, the charitable deduction would then be used. The allowable charitable deduction would be computed using the appropriate IRS tables and applicable federal rate.

Question 180: **What is a charitable lead trust?**

If your elder wants to leave an income for one of his favorite charities for a set number of years and then name a recipient for the remaining trust assets, he can use a charitable lead trust. The charity has first priority over the income interest in the trust. The trust is irrevocable and can last for a specified number of years, for your elder's life, or for the life of a specified person who must be living at the time the trust is established.

To qualify for the charitable deduction, one must set up a guaranteed annuity from the trust assets or a fixed percentage of the value of the assets. If the trust's interest income does not meet the guaranteed amount, the rest of the payment must be taken from the trust's principal. The charitable deduction is then calculated by finding the present value of the income stream using the IRS actuarial tables and the applicable federal rate.

Question 181: **What is a charitable remainder trust?**

Your elder may decide to make provisions for a portion of his remaining assets to go to charity, but he wants some other beneficiary, who is not a charity, to receive some portion of the assets first. He can do this by establishing a charitable remainder trust. Initially, the interest income would go to the noncharitable beneficiaries, and any remaining assets would go to the charity. This type of trust is irrevocable and can last for the lifetime of the named noncharity beneficiaries or for a specified number of years, which cannot exceed twenty.

In 1997, Congress added requirements to establish charitable remainder trusts that qualify for the charitable deduction. For the trust to qualify, the annuity payment in any one year cannot be more than 50 percent of the initial fair market value of the trust, or the percentage specified cannot be more than 50 percent of the trust. Also, the value of any remainder interest must be at least 10 percent of the fair market value of the trust assets on the date the trust is established. These new provisions were added to ensure that some of the trust's assets actually go to the charity.

Question 182: **What are a charitable remainder annuity trust and a charitable remainder unitrust?**

The primary difference is the way in which the ongoing payments to the beneficiaries of the trust are calculated. With a charitable remainder annuity trust (CRAT), the payment to beneficiaries is a set sum that cannot be less than 5 percent of the initial fair market value of the trust assets. With a charitable remainder unitrust (CRUT), the payments to beneficiaries are a fixed percentage that must be at least 5 percent. Any time the interest income of the trust does not meet the payout requirements, the principal of the trust must be used. A fixed percentage, such as that used in the CRUT, can be more risky if your elder wants to be certain that the principal assets are not used.

Question 183: **What are pooled income funds?**

Pooled income funds, which must be established by a public charity, are a type of charitable remainder trust that pools your elder's donated assets with others' assets. These funds are used by people who want to take advantage of the estate tax charitable deduction using a charitable remainder trust but don't have enough assets to warrant the costs of setting up an individual trust.

Your elder's will can specify that when your elder's estate transfers property to the fund, one or more individuals who are alive at the time of the transfer will get a life income interest in the property transferred. The remaining value of the property then becomes a charitable contribution; the charity involved has an irrevocable vested remainder interest in the property. The income interest paid to the named beneficiaries is paid out as a percentage of the total contributed by their donor/decedent. When the income beneficiaries die, the principal amount remaining is passed to the public charity.

Question 184: **What is a qualified funeral trust?**

Funeral expenses can be deducted from your elder's gross estate. One way to set aside these expenses while your elder is still alive and to ensure that they will be deductible is to establish a qualified funeral trust. For this trust to meet the requirements, it must:

- Result from a contract with a person in the trade or business of providing funeral or burial services
- Have the sole purpose to hold, invest, and reinvest funds in the trust and to use these funds for the sole purpose of paying for funeral or burial services for the benefit of the beneficiaries of the trust
- Permit only beneficiaries who are named in the trust to be provided services upon their death under the specified contract with the funeral company
- Be set up specifically for the purpose of a qualified funeral trust (You can't designate a trust set up for another purpose as a qualified funeral trust after the person's death to avoid taxes.)
- Be owned by the purchasers of the contract

Chapter 15

RULES ON GIFTS FROM YOUR ELDERS

YOUR ELDER MAY want to give you assets while she is still alive so that she can watch you and your family enjoy them. Be careful, because sizable gifts are not completely tax-free. In this chapter, I'll review what a gift is and the nuances of how to give a gift and minimize those taxes.

Question 185: **For tax purposes, what is a gift?**

A gift can be money or property, including the use of property without expecting to receive something of equal value in return. Your elder also may make a gift if she sells something at less than its value or makes an interest-free or reduced-interest loan. The IRS takes a very broad view of whether an asset is a gift. The federal gift tax applies to any completed direct or indirect lifetime transfer of property by a competent donor for less than the full or adequate consideration in money. That means, the IRS can determine that something is a gift even if your elder did not intend it to be. The person receiving the gift doesn't have to pay taxes on it but will have to pay taxes on any income generated by the gift. The person giving the gift may have to pay gift or estate taxes on it.

119

Certain transactions between family members can be considered gifts even if they are not intended as such. Here are some common situations that your elder must watch out for to avoid giving a gift when she doesn't intend to do so:

- Forgiveness of a legally enforceable debt—Parents often give their children a loan to go to school, buy a house, or start a business. If your elder forgave the loan, and this loan exceeds the maximum allowable amount in a given year, your elder could end up owing gift taxes.
- Intrafamily loans—People often loan money to family members at an interest rate considerably below what would be charged by a bank. If the amount of interest saved would be more than the allowable amount in a given year, your elder could end up owing gift taxes.
- Bargain sales—Sometimes an older family member decides to sell an asset to a younger family member at a price well below market value. This can be considered a bargain sale, and your elder may have to pay a gift tax on the difference between what the younger family member pays and the market value of the asset.

Currently, your elder can give up to $12,000—$24,000 as a couple—without having to worry about paying taxes on the gift. This amount is adjusted annually for inflation. Your elder can give up to $1 million cumulatively over her lifetime without having to pay gift taxes, but the amount of the gifts your elder gives will be added to the value of her gross estate.

There are some exceptions to the tax rules on gifts. The following types of gifts do not count against your elder's annual gift-giving limit:

- Tuition or medical expenses that your elder pays directly to an educational or medical institution for someone's benefit
- Gifts to her spouse

- Gifts to a political organization for its use
- Gifts to charities

If your elder gives you a gift in exchange for services, it is not considered a gift and should be reported as income. You do not have to report the receipt of a true gift on your income taxes.

Question 186: **How do I calculate the fair market value of gifts?**

Generally, the fair market value of a gift is calculated based on the value of the gift on the date of transfer. If your elder undervalues the gift on her gift tax return by 50 percent or more, she can be penalized for that undervaluation. The IRS states that the fair market value of a gift is "the price at which the property would change hands between a willing buyer and a willing seller, neither being under any compulsion to buy or to sell and both having reasonable knowledge of relevant facts. The fair market value of a particular item of property includible in the decedent's gross estate is not to be determined by a forced sale price. Nor is the fair market value of an item of property to be determined by the sale price of the item in a market other than that in which such item is most commonly sold to the public, taking into account the location of the item wherever appropriate." In other words, for most gifts, the fair market value equals the retail price at which the gift could have been purchased on the open market.

Question 187: **What are the filing requirements for gifts?**

When your elder makes a gift that is subject to the gift tax, she must file IRS Form 709. If a couple makes a gift, each person must file this form. There is no such thing as filing a gift tax return jointly. If your parents elect to split a gift that is less than two times the maximum annual exclusion amount ($24,000 in 2008), a spouse may signify consent without filing a separate form.

In addition to filing Form 709, your elder must attach these documents, if appropriate:

- Copies of transfer documents, such as deeds or trusts
- Statements from the insurance companies on Form 712, Life Insurance Statement, for each insurance policy listed on Form 709
- Financial documentation if the gift transfer involves a closely held business interest
- Professional appraisals of assets, especially if real estate is involved in the transfer

Your elder files her gift tax return on the same date as her income tax return. For example, if your elder makes a large gift in June, it does not have to be reported until April 15 of the next year. The only time this deadline may be different is if the gift tax return is being filed after your elder's death. In that case, the federal estate tax return must be filed within nine months after the death unless a six-month extension is requested. The gift tax return must be filed at the same time as the estate tax return, if it is due before April 15.

Question 188: **What are special valuations for intrafamily transfers?**

Valuation on gifts involving intrafamily transfers can be particularly difficult to prove satisfactorily to the government when they involve a closely held business. In fact, four sections of the gift and estate tax codes are concerned with how to value intrafamily transfers. Section 2701 applies specifically to transfers relating to corporate or partnership interests when there is no established market for such interests. Section 2702 applies to transfers in trust or transfers of term interests. Term interests include any interest that will last for only a specified amount of time or a lifetime. (Trusts and term interests are discussed further in Question 190.) Section 2703 applies to restrictions on the right to acquire, use, or sell property at less than fair market value or in a buy-sell agreement among business partners. (Buy-sell agreements are presented in Question 234.) Section 2704 applies to liquidation issues. If your elder is planning to make a gift to a family member, she should work with a financial adviser or attorney familiar with the intrafamily transfer laws. The government pays close attention to these types of transfers because of the valuation games some taxpayers have played. Penalties can be high if your elder doesn't value these gifts appropriately.

Question 189: **How is the valuation for purposes of gift taxes determined on lifetime transfers?**

When valuing a lifetime transfer for the purposes of gift taxes, three basic situations must exist for this type of intrafamily transfer to be legitimate:

1. There must be a gratuitous transfer, which is a transfer of property other than at fair market value.
2. The donor and the donee must be related.
3. The donor or a member of the donor's family must retain ownership interest in what is given away.

Your elder cannot use the rules of sections 2701 and 2702 if the transfer involves a sale, a transaction between strangers, or the transfer of the donor's (and all applicable family members') entire interest in the asset.

In valuing this type of transfer for the purposes of gift taxes when the donor gives only part of her interest in the asset, subtract the value of what the donor has retained from what she owned prior to the transfer. This method of determining value is called the subtraction method. Under certain conditions, the IRS can rule that the value of the property retained is zero, and your elder must pay gift taxes on the entire value of what was owned prior to the transaction. Don't try to do this type of transfer on your own. Seek professional advice.

Question 190: **How is the valuation calculated on retained interest trusts and term interests?**

When transferring interests in trust or by a term interest, the gift tax value is determined by the subtraction method, as discussed in Question 189. This does apply if the property transferred into the trust is a personal residence used by the beneficiaries of the trust. Whether the retained interests will be valued at zero or at the value found by using the subtraction method will depend on whether the interest meets the definition of a qualified interest. If the transferor and applicable family members hold control of the entity (50 percent of the stock or partnership interest), and the transferor and applicable family members retain liquidation, put, call, or conversion rights, then the retained interests are nonqualified and will be valued at zero.

For the IRS to consider that the donor or applicable family member has a retained interest of more than zero, which would mean that she has a qualified interest, the retained right must give the donor something of economic value that will be subject to estate or gift tax at some future point. The IRS wants to ensure that the entire value of the asset will be subject to transfer tax at least once.

Question 191: **What are the effects of buy-sell agreements, options, and restrictions on valuation on the gift tax?**

A buy-sell agreement can help to transfer property at less than fair market value, provided that the transfer is proven to be a bona fide business arrangement. Although this can be done more easily when strangers are involved, a buy-sell agreement also can be used with intrafamily transfers. When an intrafamily transfer is involved, your elder must prove the following:

- The arrangement isn't simply an attempt to transfer property to a family member for less than the full and adequate consideration in money.

- The terms of the agreement drafted with the family member are similar to arrangements that would be made by people in an arm's-length transaction. An arm's-length transaction is defined as a transaction between two parties that is conducted as though they were not related and there is no question of a conflict of interest.

Question 192: **What is a lifetime transfer, and when is it complete?**

A lifetime transfer is a transfer of a portion of ownership during a person's lifetime to the intended heir, but with the retention of some benefits from that asset. A lifetime transfer can be a valuable tool for closely held family businesses. Suppose your elder wants to transfer the business to her children or other family members but retains a source of income for herself and continues to consult with the successors regarding the operation of the business. This can create a problem for estate tax purposes, so it's important that it is clearly stated when your elder relinquishes all dominion and control over the gifted property (a business, trust, or other asset). As long as your elder reserves certain powers over the gift, it is not considered complete. For a lifetime transfer to be considered complete, the donor must give up the power to change beneficiaries or alter the proportionate shares of beneficiaries.

When trying to determine the value of a gift, two things must be considered: the date the gift was completed and the nature of the gifted asset. This can become very convoluted when a lifetime transfer is involved. In some situations, a person can hold an ownership interest in a completed gift. For example, if a father makes a gift of his business to his son but retains a life estate interest in the gift in the form of continuing income, it can be considered a completed gift for gift tax purposes as long as the father transfers title and all control to the son.

The timing of a gift's completion can be critical because the value of the gift will be based on the date of transfer. If your elder expects an asset to continue to increase in value, she may want to lock in the earliest possible date for transfer. If your elder doesn't complete the gift prior to her death, the transfer date for the purpose of valuing the transfer will be the date of death or six months after the death, depending on the date chosen by your elder's personal representative.

Question 193: **How does adding a child's name to property affect the gift tax?**

A common practice to avoid probate is to add a child's name to the title of property, such as the parental home. If your elder does add her child's name as a joint tenant with right of survivorship, then your elder has given her child a gift—and that gift may be subject to gift taxes if its value exceeds the maximum amount of the annual exclusion.

Another common practice is for an elderly person to add the name of a child or other relative to a joint bank account so that the younger person can help pay the bills. This means that either person has a right to the money in the account. As long as the child or other younger person put on the account only writes out checks to pay the bills of the older person, then the money will not be considered a gift. But if the younger person uses the money for himself, that amount could be subject to gift tax if it exceeds the allowable annual exclusion.

Question 194: **What is a defective disclaimer?**

You may get a gift and decide that you don't want it—either because you don't want the value of the gift to be included in your estate at death, or you want someone else to get the gift. Whatever the reason, if you get a gift you don't want, you must prepare a qualified disclaimer to refuse the gift. If you reject the gift without meeting the requirements of the IRS, you will have to pay gift or estate taxes on it when you give it to someone else. To avoid writing a defective disclaimer, you should keep in mind the key parts of a qualified disclaimer:

- You must refuse the gift in writing.
- You must refuse the gift within nine months of receiving it by sending the refusal to the donor or the legal representative of the donor.
- You must not accept the interest in the asset or any of its benefits.
- You may not have any say in who gets the asset instead of you.
- Your refusal must be irrevocable and unqualified.

Question 195: **What transfers of property are exempt from the gift tax?**

There aren't many transfers of property that are exempt from the gift tax, but a few do exist. These include:

- Transfers to political organizations
- Payments that qualify for an educational exemption (see Question 196)
- Payments that qualify for a medical exemption (see Question 197)

Medical and educational payments that qualify for the exemptions are unlimited in amount and do not have to be counted against the allowable maximum exclusion for gift tax purposes. These types of payments can be made even if your elder is not related to the person receiving the payments.

Question 196: **What qualifies as an educational exemption?**

The payment must be made on behalf of an individual to a qualifying domestic or foreign organization. In order to qualify, an organization must maintain a regular facility and curriculum and have a regularly enrolled student body in attendance where the educational activities take place. The payment also must be made directly to the institution and not to the individual for the purpose of tuition. This exemption can't be used for buying books or supplies. Nor can it be used for dormitory fees, board, or other similar expenses related to getting an education if these expenses are not direct tuition payments. Any money given, even if given directly to the institution, for other educational costs will be considered a gift and could be subject to the gift tax if the amount exceeds the allowable annual exclusion maximum.

Question 197: **What qualifies as a medical exemption?**

The payment must be made by your elder on behalf of an individual and sent directly to a medical care provider or institution that provided medical care to the individual. Medical care expenses can include diagnosis, cure, mitigation, treatment, or prevention of disease. The payment also can cover the cost of transportation primarily for and essential to the medical care. In addition, your elder can cover the costs of medical insurance for an individual, provided that your elder make the payments directly to the insurance company. Your elder cannot pay for medical care that normally would be covered by an individual's medical insurance. If your elder does make payments toward services that normally would be covered by insurance, those payments will be considered a gift and could be subject to the gift tax if the amount exceeds the allowable annual exclusion maximum.

Question 198: **How do I calculate total calendar-year gifts?**

When filing taxes for any year during which your elder gave gifts to others, make a list of those gifts. If the total gift to any one person exceeds the allowable annual exclusion maximum of $12,000, your elder will be liable for gift taxes. Since your elder is allowed to give away a total of $1 million in gifts over her lifetime without paying taxes, she will have to report the gift but won't actually have to pay any taxes unless she has exceeded her $1 million limit. Your elder can reduce her gift tax obligation even further by splitting the gift with her spouse.

Question 199: **What is the annual exclusion?**

The annual exclusion is an amount that your elder can deduct from the value of gifts in order to reduce her gift tax. Your elder gets this exclusion each year, and it is not cumulative from year to year.

In 2008, taxpayers could deduct a maximum of $12,000. The government may adjust the annual exclusion maximum on a yearly basis to reflect inflation. The adjustment must occur in multiples of $1,000, so it may take several years before the government decides to increase the exclusion amount. The last time the exclusion amount was adjusted—from $11,000, which was set in 2002, to $12,000, set in 2005—it took three years for the change to happen.

For a gift to qualify for this annual exclusion, there must be a present value to the donee. Your elder can't use the exclusion if the gift does not grant the donee present use of the money or other asset. For example, cash, a gift of a life estate in property, or a gift that involves a fee-simple interest in property could be considered gifts with present value. A gift of a remainder interest in property at some point would not qualify for the annual exclusion.

Question 200: **What are gift tax deductions?**

After your elder has taken an exclusion for each of the gifts she is allowed, she still may be able to use one of two gift tax deductions to minimize her gift tax liability: the marital deduction (to find out what qualifies, see Question 201) and the charitable deduction (to find out what qualifies, see Question 202). As with the federal estate tax, both of the deductions are unlimited and can erase your elder's gift tax liability.

Question 201: **What qualifies for the marital deduction of gift taxes?**

Your elder may give gifts to her spouse in an unlimited amount. The only limits on a marital gift involve the type of interest given. To fully qualify for the marital deduction, there are some limitations to how the gift is given:

- The couple must be married at the time of the gift. For federal tax purposes, since the Defense of Marriage Act was passed in 1996, a qualified marriage is a marriage between a man and a woman. A same-sex married couple does not qualify.
- The spouse who receives the gift must be a U.S. citizen.
- The gift must be included in your elder's total calendar-year gifts.
- Your elder cannot be given a terminable interest in the gift. A terminable interest is one that will end after a period of time or is based on some contingency. But as long as an interest in the property in question is not given to someone else, the IRS usually will allow the marital deduction.
- Your elder's spouse is given a qualified interest in the property for life.

Question 202: **What qualifies for the charitable deduction of gift taxes?**

Your elder can give millions of dollars to charity, and all of it will be free of any federal gift tax. There are no limits to the amount of money or other assets one can donate to charity as long as the charity is on the IRS list of acceptable charities. Private foundations and charitable trusts will be scrutinized more carefully by the IRS, but they still can qualify. To qualify for the charitable deduction, there are some limitations on how the money can be given:

- The gift must be cash or property. Your elder can't deduct a gift of time or talent.
- The total of the gift can be based only on any value above what your elder may have received from a charity in return.
- The transfer cannot be one of partial interest, but the gift and estate code provides for some exceptions.
- Your elder can claim a deduction only for the calendar year in which the gift was completed.
- The property for which the deduction is taken must be included in your elder's total calendar-year gifts.

Question 203: What is an inter vivos transfer (lifetime gift)?

An inter vivos transfer is any transfer of property between people who are still living. For example, if your elder gives someone her home while she is still living without retaining rights to that home, your elder is making an inter vivos transfer. This gift would no longer be part of your elder's estate at the time of her death, because she no longer owns it. To be counted as an inter vivos transfer, a gift must:

- Be given voluntarily to another person
- Be gratuitous, which means one can't have gotten anything in return
- Be accepted by the person who received the gift

Question 204: What is a testamentary transfer?

A testamentary transfer is the transfer of property or other assets through the use of a will after one's death. The property or assets remain in one's possession throughout one's lifetime.

Question 205: **What are the advantages of an inter vivos transfer?**

An inter vivos transfer can be a valuable estate-planning tool that lets your elder give property away while she is alive and can watch the recipients enjoy the gift. It also gets the property out of your elder's estate, which makes the probate process cheaper and easier. Your elder may be able to save taxes. Here are the advantages:

- Your elder can take advantage of the annual exclusion from gift and estate taxes of $12,000 per person or $24,000 per couple. This exclusion is not cumulative, and your elder can take it every year.
- The value of the gift is based on the year it is given, so your elder won't incur additional taxes based on any appreciation in value between the time your elder gives the asset to the recipient and the time of your elder's death. If your elder does not give the gift until her death, all that additional value can be taxed.
- If the gift involves the generation of taxable income, by transferring the asset to a lower-tax-bracket recipient, your elder can reduce taxes that must be paid on the income generated.
- Your elder doesn't have to pay any transfer tax on gifts until the cumulative total of gifts exceeds the applicable credit amount, which is $3.5 million in 2009. In 2010, the estate tax will be repealed, so you won't have to worry about any transfer in that year. However, the estate tax will go back to its pre-2004 state if Congress doesn't act by 2011.
- The transfer is not as public as a testamentary transfer, which must be filed with the court as part of probate.
- If done properly, your elder can protect the assets from claims by creditors.

Question 206: **What are the disadvantages of an inter vivos transfer?**

Your elder will find some disadvantages to an inter vivos transfer. The primary disadvantage is that the transfer cannot be revoked, so your elder can never get the property back. She loses all control over it. Other disadvantages include the following:

- Your elder may need to pay gift taxes out of pocket if she exceeds the annual exclusion.
- If property values decline, your elder won't be able to reduce tax liability.
- Sometimes tax laws change; your elder may find that it would have been more beneficial to give the gift at a later date.
- Your elder loses control of the property and its income.

Question 207: **What are the consequences of an outright lifetime gift?**

When doing estate planning, consider the following consequences of an outright lifetime gift:

- Your elder loses control over the asset.
- Your elder may have to pay gift taxes if the value of the gift exceeds the annual exclusion maximum.
- The asset is removed from your elder's gross estate, but its taxable portion will be used when calculating the estate taxes as an adjusted taxable gift (read Chapters 13 and 14 for more information on this point).
- The donee will be responsible for any taxes for capital gains from the time he receives the asset until the time it is sold.
- The donee will need to report any income generated from the gift and pay taxes on it.

- The gifted asset will be taxed as part of the donee's estate if still owned, or the donee could have to pay gift taxes on the asset if he gives it away before his death.

Question 208: **What is an outright total-interest charitable gift?**

Your elder can give total interest in an asset to a charitable organization and get a charitable gift tax deduction, as well as a limited charitable income tax deduction. The charity must be on the list of qualified charities published by the IRS, and the gift must be in the form of cash or property. In order for a gift to qualify as an outright total-interest charitable gift, your elder must give fee-simple title to the cash or property.

Question 209: **What is a charitable bargain sale?**

Your elder can sell an asset to charity for less than its market value on the date of the sale and then take a charitable gift tax deduction for the difference between the sale price and the fair market value of the asset less the annual exclusion. This is called a charitable bargain sale.

Question 210: **What is a charitable stock bailout?**

A charitable stock bailout involves the donation to charity of a closely held stock. The donor gets a charitable gift tax deduction for the fair market value of the stock less the annual exclusion. In most cases, the stock will be redeemed by the privately held corporation for cash, since the charity wants the cash, and the remaining stockholders in this closely held company probably don't want a charity as a co-owner.

In order for this gift to qualify as a charitable stock bailout, your elder cannot make a formal or informal agreement that the corporation will redeem the stock. In most cases, a person chooses to use a charitable stock bailout to avoid paying capital gains that would be due if the stock were sold. The remaining shareholders increase their percentage of ownership by redeeming the shares.

Question 211: **What is a charitable gift annuity?**

A charitable gift annuity is a gift to a charity of a set amount per year during one's lifetime. The actuarial value of this gift will be less than a cash donation or an outright donation of property because the gift will be given over a number of years. To calculate the charitable deduction for a charitable gift annuity, one would need to figure out the difference between the annuity and an outright cash gift and then subtract that difference less an annual exclusion.

The donor can name himself as the annuitant, or he can name his spouse, and he won't have to pay any tax on the present value of the annuity. If he names his spouse, any interest given to her would qualify for a marital deduction. If anyone other than the donor or the spouse is named, the present value of the annuity is subject to gift tax. The donor can keep a portion of the gifted annuity as income, so this type of annuity is similar to a charitable remainder trust (see Question 181), but the advantage of using this type of annuity is that one doesn't have to go through the expense of setting up a trust.

Question 212: **What is an outright partial-interest charitable gift?**

Your elder can get a charitable gift tax deduction even if she gives a qualified charity only a partial interest in her personal residence or farm. A personal residence can include any interest in real property, such as a vacation home or time-share, as long as the property is used as at least a part-time residence. Interestingly, even the remainder interest in a yacht can qualify, as long as the yacht is used as a part-time residence. A farm is defined as any land used by the donor for the production of crops, fruit, or other agricultural products, or for the care and feeding of livestock.

Your elder can take the charitable gift tax deduction even if the charity's only interest is that it gets to take possession of the property involved after the donor's death or the death of someone named to have a life estate. For example, a husband can donate property and give his wife the right to life on the property until her death. After her death, the property would go to the charity.

Question 213: **What is an intrafamily loan?**

Anytime your elder makes a loan to a family member at no interest or at an interest rate below the applicable federal rate as set by the IRS, she is considered to have made a gift to the person who gets the loan. The amount of the interest that is not collected is considered your elder's income, even though she doesn't get any cash. The uncollected cash, known as "imputed interest," is subject to gift tax.

Your elder doesn't have to worry about imputed interest if the loan is less than $10,000 and is used to purchase non–income-producing property. Your elder also doesn't have to worry about loans up to $100,000 for the purposes of buying business property, as long as the borrower's net investment income is less than $1,000. Any imputed interest on this business loan is limited to the net investment interest income over $1,000. The borrower can deduct actual interest paid but cannot deduct the imputed interest amount.

Question 214: **What is a custodial gift?**

If your elder doesn't want to incur the cost of setting up and maintaining a trust but she does want to have some control of the assets, a custodial gift can be an excellent alternative. Custodial gifts are simple to set up and don't involve the payment of many fees.

Your elder can administer the property, or she can name a third party, such as a bank representative, to administer the gift. A custodial gift is not a true trust, because the minor beneficiary has both legal and equitable title to the property. But custodial gifts can function in a similar way to irrevocable trusts. The primary reason one saves money on this type of gift is that trust documents don't have to be drawn up and executed. In fact, no document is necessary because the property is administered according to laws set up in each state under the Uniform Gifts to Minors Act.

Question 215: **What is the Uniform Gifts to Minors Act?**

Each state has its own version of the Uniform Gifts to Minors Act (UGMA) or the Uniform Transfers to Minors Act (UTMA). Many states started with the UGMA but switched to the UTMA. Here are the differences:

- The UGMA allows gifts of only cash, securities, and life insurance; the UTMA does not restrict the type of property one can give.
- The UGMA allows one to make lifetime transfers only; the UTMA allows one to make transfers to the trust during one's lifetime or as part of one's will.
- The custodian of an UTMA has greater investment and management powers than the custodian of an UGMA.

In order to contribute to an UGMA or UTMA, one simply titles the asset in the name of a competent adult who will serve as the custodian for the benefit of the minor beneficiary based on the statutes of the state. For example, if your elder wants to set up a trust for her grandchild, she can name you (the child's parent) as the trustee. One must set up a separate UGMA or UTMA account for each minor.

Question 216: **What are the elements of a gift in trust?**

A more complex way to leave money to a minor or other person is to leave it as a gift in trust. A trust has five elements:

1. The person granting the trust must be legally competent, as defined by state law. The person granting the trust can be called a grantor, settlor, or trustor.

2. The trustee, the person who manages the trust, must be legally competent. The trustee holds a legal interest in all trust property.

3. The beneficiary (there can be more than one beneficiary) holds an equitable or beneficial interest in the property. The beneficiary can be classified as an income or remainder beneficiary. An income beneficiary enjoys current income from the trust. A remainder beneficiary gets all assets left over when the trust ends. Most trusts are set up with a term limit.

4. The property given to the trust is called the *trust corpus* or principal. Usually, the grantor contributes most of the property in the trust, but property can be contributed by others. In some states, the trust corpus is titled in the trustee's name; in other states, the corpus is held in the name of the trustee acting in a fiduciary capacity.

5. The trustee has a fiduciary relationship with the beneficiaries of the trust. The trustee's fiduciary responsibilities include investing the assets and managing the trust property in the best interests of the trust beneficiaries. He also has the responsibility to distribute the assets according to the terms of the trust.

Chapter 16

USING TRUSTS TO GET YOUR ELDER'S ESTATE IN ORDER

TRUSTS CAN BE an excellent way to work with your elder to get his finances in order. They also can be used to minimize probate costs and taxes on the transfer of assets. In this chapter, I'll review many of the key types of trusts and how they are used.

Question 217: **What are the goals of a trust?**

Trustors set up trusts with numerous goals in mind, including the following:

- Allowing the trust assets to benefit numerous beneficiaries at the same time. A trust can be set up so that some people get income during their lifetimes while others get the corpus of the trust when the term ends.
- Providing professional management of the funds, which can be particularly important if the beneficiary of the trust is a minor child or a mentally incompetent adult. Also, professional management can be useful if the

beneficiaries are not experienced with investing money or managing property.

- Avoiding probate by funding the trust while still alive.
- Protecting assets from the grantor's creditors, as long as the trust is set up as an irrevocable trust. If the assets in an irrevocable trust are set up with a spendthrift provision, they can be protected from the beneficiaries' creditors, as well.
- Saving gift taxes by splitting the income among multiple beneficiaries. One can also qualify for multiple annual exclusions and valuation discounts. One also reduces estate taxes by eliminating assets from one's gross estate (one can only eliminate taxes if one sets up an irrevocable trust with no retained interest).

Question 218: **What is a minor's trust?**

Your elder can set up a minor's trust if he wants to give property to a minor but wants the property to be administered by someone else until that minor is mature enough to handle the responsibility of managing the property. Your elder probably doesn't want the trust to make mandatory income payments to the minor child. A minor's trust is usually set up with income distribution at the discretion of the trustee, which means the minor will not have a present interest in the trust, and the grantor will not be able to take advantage of annual gift tax exclusions. Your elder can set up the trust giving the minor present interest, but then the minor may have access to large sums of money earlier than intended.

Question 219: **What are qualified tuition plans?**

To set aside money for their children, many parents use qualified tuition plans, also known as 529 plans because they were established by Section 529 of the IRS code. These plans can be set up for the benefit of any person, including a minor, provided that there is an approved sponsor. Approved sponsors include both private and public entities. Account balances grow tax free, and there is no required age for distribution.

The beneficiary of an account can be changed. For example, suppose your elder sets up a 529 for a child, but that child decides not to go to college. Your elder can then change the named beneficiary to another child, such as a niece, nephew, or grandchild.

Today, there are two types of 529 plans on the market. Some are set up by specific educational institutions. These are used to purchase prepaid tuition credits and are known as prepaid plans. Other types of 529 plans invest in mutual funds. In most cases, your elder is better off selecting a type of plan that invests in mutual funds rather than one that is tied to a specific educational institution.

Your elder can contribute up to $12,000 per year per person into a 529 plan, and the gift will qualify for a gift tax exclusion, just like other gifts. But 529s have a special provision that allows your elder to contribute up to $60,000 in one year because the contributions can be taxed as though they were made over a five-year period. Thus all of this single contribution could qualify for five years of annual exclusions and be completely exempt from the gift tax.

Question 220: **What are Coverdell Education Savings Accounts?**

Another type of educational savings account is the Coverdell Education Savings Account (ESA), which is a trust or custodial account created solely for the purpose of paying qualified educational expenses of the designated beneficiary of the account. When the account is first established, the designated beneficiary must be under age eighteen or have special needs. Your elder must establish the account specifically as a Coverdell ESA when he first opens it. The conditions for setting up the account include:

- The account must be set up with a trustee or custodian that is a bank or other entity approved by the IRS.

- Contributions must be in cash and must be made before the beneficiary reaches age eighteen, unless the beneficiary is a special-needs beneficiary.
- One cannot contribute more than $2,000 per year.
- One cannot invest the money in the account in life insurance contracts.
- One cannot combine the money in the account with other property except in a common trust fund or common investment fund.
- The balance in the account must be distributed within thirty days after the beneficiary reaches age thirty—unless the beneficiary is a special-needs beneficiary—or the beneficiary's death, whichever comes first.

Your elder can set up a Coverdell ESA even if he already has a Section 529 plan in place. Funds in a Coverdell ESA grow tax free but can be used only for qualified educational expenses, including tuition and fees, books, supplies, equipment, and academic tutoring.

Question 221: **What is a support trust?**

If your elder has the obligation to support someone else, he may set up an irrevocable support trust either by choice or by court mandate. For example, in a divorce situation, the noncustodial parent can be required to fund an irrevocable trust with enough assets to guarantee that the child support payments will be made. Another common use of this kind of trust would be to provide long-term support for an incapacitated person.

A professional whose assets could potentially be seized by judgment creditors also may use an irrevocable support trust to protect those assets. For example, a doctor who could be sued for malpractice may use this kind of trust to protect his assets. The trust must be irrevocable in order to provide a shield from creditors.

With a support trust, the trustee has discretion over the distribution of both the principal and the interest income for the health, education, maintenance, and support of the beneficiary. To protect the trust assets from claims from the beneficiary's creditors, your elder must add a spendthrift provision to the trust.

If your elder establishes a support trust, it may be subject to gift tax in the year it is established, but your elder won't be able to take an annual exclusion because the distributions of the trust are at the discretion of the trustee. Any income distributed to the beneficiary would be taxed, and the trust would pay tax on any accumulated income not given to the beneficiary.

Question 222: **What is a revocable trust?**

If your elder sets up a revocable trust, he can amend the trust's terms during his lifetime. This type of trust provides no tax benefit and does not protect the assets from creditors, so its only purposes include the following:

- Avoiding probate by placing assets in a will substitute
- Providing a mechanism to handle the grantor's affairs in case the grantor becomes incompetent or incapacitated
- Providing a mechanism for a pour-over trust (see Question 225) after the grantor's death

Your elder doesn't have to worry about gift taxes upon funding the trust. Since he retains the right to revoke the trust, it is not a completed gift.

Question 223: **What is the best way to use a contingent (standby) trust?**

This type of revocable trust is set up to establish a mechanism for your elder's funds to be handled if your elder becomes incompetent or needs to be away from home for an extended period. The primary difference in establishing a contingent trust is that your elder funds the trust with very little money at the time it is created. Instead of fully funding the trust initially, your elder attaches a durable power of attorney to the trust, which gives someone the authority to transfer your elder's assets into the trust if the named contingency happens. Often the person who has the power of attorney also will be the person named as the trustee.

For example, suppose your elder establishes this trust when he is well, but he knows that at some point his illness (such as Alzheimer's disease) will result in the inability to handle his own affairs. Your elder would set up the trust and include a power of attorney. The power of attorney must specify how to determine whether circumstances meet the contingency, which in this example would be incompetency. Sometimes the test of whether the contingency is met will be at the sole discretion of the named trustee, but often it will be by the concurrence of one or more physicians.

In addition to establishing the contingency and how the timing of the contingency will be determined, the trust also names beneficiaries for any assets remaining in the trust after your elder's death. Your elder should include the right to revoke the trust so that he can avoid the payment of any gift tax.

Question 224: **What are distributional trusts?**

Although every type of trust has as one of its goals the proper administration and distribution of the trust's assets, several types of trust make this their primary purpose. The two most common types of distribution trusts are pour-over trusts (see Question 225) and dynasty trusts (see Question 226). These trusts don't have other goals to meet, unlike other types of trusts, such as a contingent trust, which provides support after a person becomes unable to handle his affairs, or a support trust (see Question 221), which is set up to provide support for someone.

Question 225: **What is a pour-over trust?**

A pour-over trust is established during one's lifetime as a place to put all of one's assets and then distribute them to multiple beneficiaries. It gets its name because assets are "poured" into the trust from numerous sources such as one's will, life insurance proceeds, pension or profit-sharing plans, and other assets.

By establishing this type of trust, your elder can avoid probate (except for assets that are put into the trust after his death). A pour-over trust can prevent a second probate for assets that are left over because they were not distributed based on the terms of your elder's will. Otherwise any remaining assets at the end of probate would need to go through a second probate to determine what to do with them. In many cases, a pour-over trust is a revocable living trust that continues after your elder's death.

Question 226: **What is a dynasty trust?**

A dynasty trust is a type of trust that can be used to pass one's assets to several generations of beneficiaries. Since any transfer to people who are two or more generations younger than your elder can be subject to the generation-skipping transfer tax (GSTT—see Chapter 12), this type of trust can be used to minimize that tax by taking advantage of the GSTT exemption. If set up properly, the trust can use the exemption to prevent the payment of GSTT each time it passes from one generation to the next.

To avoid the GSTT, your elder must create an irrevocable dynasty trust for the benefit of his descendants and fund the trust with property that he has allocated to all or part of his GSTT exemption. If your elder sets up the trust in this way, the property will be subject to gift taxes only.

Most states put a time limit on dynasty trusts, but some states allow these funds to transfer in perpetuity. The states that let a person set up perpetual trusts are Alaska, Arizona, Delaware, Idaho, Illinois, Maryland, South Dakota, and Wisconsin. Other states allow such a long lifespan that the trusts can almost be considered perpetual. For example, Wyoming allows one to establish a trust for 1,000 years, and Florida permits trusts to be established for 360 years. Your elder doesn't have to live in a state to establish a trust there. If he does want to establish a trust, make sure that he does so in a state that meets his long-range plans.

Other advantages of the dynasty trust include:

- Protection of the assets from lawsuits during the descendant's lifetime, as long as properly drafted spendthrift provisions are added to the trust documents, which will limit the amount of money that can be taken out in any one year
- Administrative and tax savings during probate
- Prevention of the assets' becoming marital property of the descendant, so they cannot be subject to claims by a beneficiary's spouse during a divorce

Question 227: **What is a mandatory income trust?**

If your elder wants to provide income annually to beneficiaries and take advantage of the gift tax annual exclusion, he can set up a mandatory income trust. This type of trust can be funded while one is alive or after one's death. To qualify for the annual gift tax exclusions, however, your elder must fund it while he is alive.

Your elder can name multiple income beneficiaries and use the annual gift tax exclusion ($12,000 in 2008) for each beneficiary. (The IRS can adjust the exclusion maximum for inflation—see Question 199.) The income beneficiaries have a present interest in the trust, and annual income must be paid out each year.

In addition to income beneficiaries, your elder also can name remainder beneficiaries, who will get any principal left in the trust when the trust ends. There is no mandatory time at which this type of trust must end, but state law will limit the trust from being established in perpetuity unless the trust is set up in a state that allows perpetual trusts. Those states are Alaska, Arizona, Delaware, Idaho, Illinois, Maryland, South Dakota, and Wisconsin. As with dynasty trusts, some states allow these trusts to be set up with such a long lifespan as to make them, in effect, perpetual. Your elder doesn't have to live in a state to establish a trust there, so make sure that he chooses a state that meets his long-range plans.

Question 228: **What is a Crummey trust?**

Your elder can use a Crummey trust to take advantage of the annual gift tax exclusion by giving his grandchild money each year but not actually giving the grandchild cash. For a lifetime gift to be eligible for the annual gift tax exclusion, the grandchild must have a present interest; however, the Crummey trust allows your elder to control that interest. The trust is named for the Crummey family, who took the IRS to court to win the right to restrict their children from taking money out of a trust at too young an age.

This type of trust gives a grandchild the right to withdraw a gift thirty days after the gift is made. While the grandchild is young, your elder doesn't have to worry about her taking money from the trust. The trust meets the gift tax law by giving her a present interest, but she won't be old enough to know that she can take the money. As she gets older, if she decides to withdraw an annual gift, your elder can stop making annual gifts to the trust.

After the thirty-day window for withdrawal, the grandchild cannot access the funds until the age that your elder sets for distribution. This can be whatever age your elder chooses. Many families arrange for distributions at several different ages.

A Crummey trust offers more control over the money for a longer period than a custodial gift does (see Question 214). Children generally are allowed all access to the money at the age of 21; some states permit access as young as 18.

Question 229: **What is a grantor-retained annuity trust?**

By establishing a grantor-retained annuity trust (GRAT), your elder can ensure that he'll receive an annuity amount from the trust at least annually. Usually, this annuity is set up based on a fixed percentage of the initial value of the trust assets. The payment of the trust can increase each year, but not by more than 120 percent of the previous year's amount.

A GRAT is an irrevocable trust funded while one is still alive. Usually, these trusts are set up for a specific amount of time, and in most cases, the grantor intends to outlive the terms of the trust. When the trust ends, its assets are distributed to the remaining beneficiaries. If the grantor dies before the term of the trust ends, any remaining funds in trust are included in the grantor's gross estate.

The present value of the remainder interest in the trust may be subject to gift tax. Compute the fair market value of the retained annuity interest; then deduct the value from the total trust assets to determine the amount of assets subject to the gift tax.

Question 230: **What is a grantor-retained unitrust?**

A grantor-retained unitrust is similar to a GRAT (see Question 229), with one twist. Your elder can set up the amount to be received as an annual annuity based on a fixed percentage of the net fair market value of the trust assets as valued annually. The amount to be paid out can be greater than the annuity amount or trust amount. The amount to be paid will vary each year based on the value of the trust assets. This type of trust can provide better protection for the assets; if the fair market value drops dramatically because of a change in the underlying assets (such as a drop in the stock market), the annuity will be reduced to avoid using up the assets too quickly.

The present value of the remainder interest in the trust may be subject to gift tax. Compute the fair market value of the retained annuity interest using different tables from those used for the

GRAT, to allow for the unitrust twist. Then deduct the value from the total trust assets to determine the amount of assets subject to the gift tax.

Question 231: **What is a grantor-retained interest (or income) trust?**

Your elder can set up a grantor-retained interest (or income) trust to provide the greatest protection for the trust corpus, because the annual annuity from the trust is based solely on the income produced by the trust. If the income goes down, the annuity goes down. If no income is generated in a particular year, no annuity will be paid from the trust. This trust will be subject to the highest gift tax and is seldom used in estate planning.

Question 232: **What is a qualified personal residence trust?**

If your elder wants to stay in his house and set up a trust to gift the assets while still alive, your elder can set up a qualified personal residence trust (QPRT). Your elder will retain the right to live in the personal residence for the term of the trust. His present value in the trust will be his right to use the residence.

Determine any gift taxes by multiplying an income factor determined by the IRS times the fair market value of the residence. Subtract this income portion of the value from the full value of the assets at the time of funding to determine the portion of the value that will be subject to gift taxes.

Chapter 17

WORKING WITH YOUR ELDER TO TRANSFER THE FAMILY BUSINESS

TRANSFERRING THE FAMILY business can be difficult, and the IRS doesn't make the process any easier. In this chapter, I'll review strategies you can consider to facilitate the transfer of a family business.

Question 233: **How does an elder transfer the business to a family member?**

Before transferring a business to a family member, your elder may need to make some changes to its structure, especially if your elder doesn't want to gift or sell the entire business at one time. If the business is a sole proprietorship, your elder will need to change the structure to a form of business that allows multiple owners. This new form can be a partnership, a limited liability company, or a corporation.

Once the new structure is in place, your elder can then gift or sell interests in the partnership or shares of stock in the corporation. If your elder wants to continue to control the business even though he plans to gift or sell part of it to one or more family members, he will need to hold on to the majority of the shares that have voting power in making company decisions.

Question 234: **What are buy-sell agreements?**

One of the best ways to deal with the issues surrounding the transfer of a closely held business is to set up a buy-sell agreement at the time the business is formed. This type of agreement can take one of two forms:

1. **Cross-purchase agreement**—The business partners set up a contract to purchase the business from each other under specified circumstances, such as death, total disability, or retirement.
2. **Entity-purchase agreement**—Each business owner contracts with the business rather than with the other owner(s). The business entity has the obligation to purchase the person's share under specified circumstances, such as death, total disability, or retirement.

Whichever agreement exists, the key is that a mechanism will be in place for valuing the business. For example, the owners could agree on a formula that combines the book value of the assets as well as the good will established over the years of running the business. Also, the process for buying the partner out of the business will be established.

Even if a buy-sell agreement is in place, review the agreement and the process for buying out a partner. The partners in the business should be certain that the agreement reflects current family situations, as well as current market conditions. If after a review, the partners think that they need to revise the agreement, it's much easier to do when there isn't the stress that might arise if one of the specific circumstances come to pass.

Question 235: **What are restrictions upon transfer?**

Many times a closely held business will put restrictions on the transfer of any stock. These restrictions will give the remaining shareholders the right to buy the shares if one of the partners wants to sell before those shares can be offered to a third party not currently an owner in the company.

Although restrictions upon transfer offer some protection to the shareholders, they do not guarantee that a problem won't arise when one of the partners wants to sell his shares and get out of the business. These restrictions usually do not establish a purchase price or a mechanism for setting one. Also, they do not establish a process for arranging what could be a sizable purchase for the remaining stockholders.

Question 236: **What are the gift tax implications?**

If your elder decides to give away a portion of his business as a gift to a family member, the gift may be subject to gift taxes. Your elder should value the transfer of corporate or partnership interests by subtracting the value of the interest he retains from the value of the interests held by all family members prior to the transfer. In most cases, the retained interests are valued as zero if:

- Immediately before the transfer, he and any applicable family members hold control of the entity and retain a distribution right that does not have the right to receive qualified payments. Qualified payments are payments that are fixed in time and amount. Applicable family members include your elder's spouse, your elder's ancestors, your elder's spouse's ancestors, and the spouses of any ancestors.
- Your elder or applicable family members retain a liquidation, put, call, or conversion right.

If your elder's retained interests are valued at zero by the IRS, then his gift taxes will be much higher.

Question 237: **What are the estate tax implications?**

When calculating estate taxes after your elder's death, you can include in his gross estate only the business interest that your elder still holds at the time of his death. If the transfer of the business to other family members took place during your elder's lifetime and the transfer resulted in taxable gifts, then the taxable gifts will become adjusted taxable gifts when the owner's estate tax is calculated. The value is adjusted based on the value when the transfer was completed.

Question 238: **What are the income tax implications?**

Your elder won't have to worry about any income tax implications if he gifts the business to family members rather than selling it. As long as your elder's interests in the business were gifted, he does not have to recognize any capital gains.

What happens instead is that there will be a carryover basis from the owner to the donee family members. Both the original business owner and the donee family members will have to report income that can be attributed to their individual shares in the company.

Question 239: **What are the nontax implications?**

Your elder must also consider the nontax implications of making a transfer of part of his business assets to a family member. The good news is that now your elder will have family member donees who will take more of an interest in the operation of the business, if for no other reason than to protect their income.

Your elder can prepare the family members who become involved in the business to take over when he retires or dies. Family members who are gifted a portion of the business may become more interested in purchasing shares at some point in the future. Your elder may then want to set up a buy-sell agreement to arrange for the transfer of any remaining assets. A gift of a portion of your elder's business may now make it a salable asset, whereas before he might have had trouble finding a buyer.

The bad news is that if your elder's donee family members disagree with how your elder runs the business, your elder may end up with a lot of arguments that he didn't have before. But as long as your elder holds the majority ownership, he will stay in control.

Chapter **18**

PLANNING LIFE INSURANCE NEEDS WITH YOUR ELDER

LIFE INSURANCE CAN help generate the cash needed to pay taxes without having to sell assets from a person's estate. It also can help to provide an ongoing income for survivors. In this chapter, I will take a quick look at the types of insurance policies you my want to consider for your elder if she doesn't already have them.

Question 240: What are the key reasons to use life insurance as an estate-planning tool?

One of the first things a financial planner will do when beginning to work on a person's estate plan is to review the life insurance policies in force. Life insurance policies are critical to anyone's estate plan for a number of reasons:

- **Estate liquidity**—All estates, whether large or small, need cash to pay any taxes, administrative costs, and debts left by the decedent. If there is a closely held business, cash also is needed to keep the business operating during probate and to pay an allowance to surviving family members during the time the estate is being administered. Life insurance proceeds can fill this cash gap quickly.

- **Retirement of debt**—The loss of the deceased person's paycheck or Social Security check can be devastating to a family's budget. A life insurance policy can retire major debts, such as the mortgage on a home.
- **Replacement of income**—Life insurance policy proceeds can be used to fund an income stream for one's family after one's death.
- **Wealth accumulation**—One can use life insurance as a means to increase one's family wealth after the death of a family member.

Question 241: **What is a joint-life policy?**

A joint-life insurance policy covers more than one life. For example, suppose your elder owns a business and wants to protect its assets. She can buy a joint-life policy with her business partner and specify that the face value of the policy will be paid to the surviving owner. In this case, the surviving owner would likely use the funds to buy out the family members of the partner who died. Another type of provision may specify that the face value of the insurance will be paid to certain beneficiaries after both people covered by the policy die.

Question 242: **What is a first-to-die policy?**

A first-to-die policy can be used in either a personal or a business situation. The policy terms specify that the face amount of the policy will be paid out upon the death of the first of one or more covered persons. For example, if your elder owns a business and uses this type of policy to protect the business assets, the life insurance proceeds will likely be used to fund a buy-sell agreement (see Question 234).

A married couple might use this type of policy rather than funding two policies to cover each of their lives separately. The face value is paid out to the surviving spouse when the first spouse dies. Life insurance proceeds at the death of the first spouse can be used to pay off a mortgage, fund grandchildren's education, replace any lost income of the person who died, or pay any estate taxes due. For example, your father could have a pension that ends upon his death, so the life insurance policy could be used to replace that income for your mother if she survives him.

Premiums on first-to-die life insurance policies are usually higher than the premiums on policies covering only one person, but the premiums are lower than the cost of carrying two or more individual life insurance policies.

Question 243: **What is a second-to-die policy?**

A second-to-die, or survivorship, policy is used by a couple. It doesn't pay anything when the first person dies but instead pays the face value of the insurance at the time the second person who is covered dies. Your parents may decide to use this policy to take full advantage of the unlimited marital deduction on their assets and use the proceeds of the second-to-die policy to fund the payment of estate taxes, so their children aren't stuck with a huge tax bill.

The premium for a second-to-die policy is lower than the cost of two separate policies. This type of policy also might make sense if one of your parents is substantially older or more expensive to insure because of illness or other factors. With this type of policy, underwriting will focus primarily on the status of the person who is likely to die last.

Question 244: **What are settlement options?**

After a person dies, the ways in which money is paid out to the beneficiaries are called settlement options. Your elder can specify how she wants the proceeds to be paid out, or she can leave that decision up to the beneficiaries.

In most cases, life insurance death benefits are paid to beneficiaries in a lump sum, in installments, or in an interest-only option. Usually, life insurance benefits received in a lump sum are tax free to the recipient. If your elder or the beneficiary she names decides that the money will be paid in installments, any interest received on money not paid out immediately will be subject to income tax.

If your elder specifies that the beneficiary should be paid only the interest generated by the insurance company on the death proceeds, and the death proceeds are paid out at a future date, then the total amount of the interest-only payments will be taxable income to the beneficiary.

Question 245: **What types of ownership can an elder have in a life insurance policy?**

The ownership of an insurance policy can have great gift and estate tax consequences. Here is a list of the possible types of ownership:

- **Right to** name and change the beneficiary
- **Right to** cash in, surrender, or cancel a policy
- **Right to** receive policy dividends
- **Right to** borrow against the cash values of the policy
- **Right to** pledge the policy as collateral for a loan
- **Right to** assign any of the foregoing rights or the policy itself
- **Right to** revoke any assignment of the rights

If your elder dies with even one of these rights to any life insurance policy on the life of another person, the replacement value of that policy must be included in your elder's gross estate. But if the owner, the insured, and the decedent are all the same person, the death benefit is included in calculation of the gross estate. If your elder transfers her ownership of the life insurance policy to someone else during the last three years of her life, the death benefit also will be included in the gross estate.

Question 246: **What is a beneficiary designation?**

All life insurance policies permit the owner to designate who will get the death benefits of the policy. The beneficiary designation permits one to name the beneficiary or beneficiaries when the policy is purchased.

When your elder is trying to decide whom to name as a beneficiary or beneficiaries on a life insurance policy, she should first consider how this policy fits into her estate plan and how it will help her meet the goals of that plan. If the primary purpose of buying that policy is to help cover any costs after your elder's death, encourage her to name somcone who is concerned with how the estate taxes or administrative costs of probate will be paid.

Question 247: **What is group term life insurance?**

When one gets life insurance through work, the policy likely is a group term life insurance policy. This is a common fringe benefit in the workplace. An employer commonly establishes a face value to the term life policy that is usually equal to one year's salary or a set dollar amount.

A group term life insurance policy is owned by the employer. One's only right to ownership is the right to name a beneficiary or beneficiaries. In some cases, one will be allowed to convert the policy to an individual policy if one leaves the job.

Any premiums the employer pays can be deducted as a business expense. The cost of coverage for the first $50,000 of life insurance benefits is not taxable income for the employee, even if it is paid by the employer. The cost of any coverage paid by the employer for a death benefit in excess of $50,000 is taxable income to employees. For example, if an employer pays for life insurance coverage up to $50,000, all premiums are nontaxable. But if the employer pays for a life insurance policy that gives someone $55,000 coverage, the difference of the cost between the $50,000 premium and the $55,000 premium would be taxable. That premium difference would be added to the employee's income for the year and taxed at current tax rates.

The death benefit from a group term life insurance policy will be included when calculating the gross estate of your elder, as long as your elder had the right to name the beneficiary. The death benefit will not be included in your elder's gross estate if the ownership of the policy was given to someone else more than three years before her death, but the gift of policy ownership may be subject to gift tax.

Question 248: **If an elder has only group term life insurance, what are her options?**

First, have your elder check with the company that issued the policy to see if there are any provisions for converting the group policy into an individual policy. Sometimes that can be done for a smaller face value, but usually it cannot.

If your elder finds out that she has no life insurance once the group policy coverage ends, she may want to consider group insurance through an association policy, such as AARP or AAA. These types of group policies probably are easier to get and have cheaper premium rates than those she will find if she tries to get individual life insurance.

If your elder decides to get individual life insurance, make sure that she gets a policy with a guaranteed payment term. Term life insurance policy rates jump rapidly once a person is over the age of 55, so if your elder can lock in a rate before she turns 50, she can save a lot on premium costs.

Question 249: **What is split-dollar life insurance?**

In a split-dollar life insurance policy, an employer and employee sign a written agreement that specifies how they will share the cost of a life insurance policy, as well as how the proceeds of the policy will be shared when the policy is surrendered either at the death of the employee or the termination of employment. These types of policies are usually offered only to extremely valuable employees.

In most cases, the employer pays the premiums that go toward increasing the cash surrender value of the policy, while the employee pays the portion of the policy that buys the death benefit. Generally, these agreements specify that the employer will receive any cash surrender value of the policy, and the employee's beneficiaries will receive the death benefit.

Either the employee or the employer can be the owner of the split-dollar life insurance policy. If the policy is owned by the employee, the employer secures his interest in the proceeds by having the employee sign a collateral assignment of the policy to the employer. If the policy is owned by the employer, he endorses the policy to allow the employee to designate the beneficiary of the portion of the life insurance proceeds granted to the employee under the agreement.

Unless your elder continues to work, she likely won't remain on a split-dollar life insurance policy. Your elder could be in a consulting position with a former employer or with a small business that she sold, so you should find out if your elder is, or was, on a split-dollar policy to see if there could be any benefits at the time of her death.

Question 250: **What is key-person life insurance?**

Businesses purchase key-person life insurance on the life of an employee who is key to the success of the business. The primary reason for this insurance is to replace the anticipated loss of income generated after the death of the key employee. In many cases, the insured employee is also an owner of the closely held business that purchased the life insurance.

Many closely held small businesses will use this type of life insurance policy to fund a buy-sell agreement (see Question 234). For example, if your elder is a partner in a small business, a key-person life insurance policy may be in place. If so, when your elder dies, the proceeds of the life insurance policy can be used to finance the buyout of your elder's stock. The money can then be used to pay any estate taxes, funeral expenses, and administrative expenses. The proceeds from a key-person life insurance policy do not have to be included in the estate of the insured so long as no part of the proceeds is payable to a personal beneficiary.

250 ELDERCARE QUESTIONS

Chapter 1: Getting Started—What Comes First?

Question 1: How do I start talking with my elderly parents?

Question 2: What are the key topics I need to talk about?

Question 3: What are the key legal documents an elder should have in place?

Question 4: What key financial planning steps should you take with an elder?

Question 5: Do I need help with estate planning?

Question 6: What types of advisers should I seek out?

Question 7: How do I find the right advisers?

Chapter 2: Taking the Right Steps to Communicate

Question 8: How do I preserve an elder's autonomy but take the control I need to take?

Question 9: What types of communication work best to get an elder's attention?

Question 10: How can I avoid trying to take over and causing conflict?

Question 11: How can I make a deal with an elder to solve a problem in a way that satisfies both our interests?

Question 12: When should I seek help in trying to communicate with an elder?

Question 13: What type of help with communication might I seek?

Question 14: How do I find the right type of adviser to help improve communication with an elder?

Chapter 3: Talking about and Planning for Incompetency

Question 15: How do I plan for the management of an elder's affairs should he or she become incompetent in the future?

Question 16: What is a joint convenience checking account?

Question 17: What is a durable power of attorney?

Question 18: What is a funded revocable living trust?

Question 19: What is a contingent (standby) trust?

Question 20: What is a special needs/Craven trust?

Question 21: What is voluntary, limited conservatorship?

Chapter 4: Problems of Incompetency

Question 22: Who can be considered incompetent?

Question 23: Why don't people plan for incompetency?

Question 24: What are state-mandated court-ordered arrangements for people to handle the financial affairs of an incompetent person?

Question 25: What is guardianship, and how does it work?

Question 26: What is conservatorship, and how does it work?

Question 27: How do I establish a guardianship or conservatorship?

Question 28: What are the powers and limits of guardianship and conservatorship?

Question 29: What are limited guardianships?

Question 30: What are limited conservatorships?

Question 31: What are the advantages of guardianships and conservatorships?

Question 32: What are the disadvantages of guardianships and conservatorships?

Chapter 5: Legal Documents You Need to Handle Your Elder's Medical Needs

Question 33: What are living wills?

Question 34: What is informed consent?

Question 35: What is substituted judgment?

Question 36: Why designate another person to make medical decisions?

Question 37: What is a proxy appointment?

Question 38: What is a medical power of attorney?

Question 39: What is a medical-decision-making agent?

Question 40: What are medical directives?

Question 41: What is a do-not-resuscitate order?

Chapter 6: Assessing Your Elder's Income and Budget

Question 42: How do I determine how much income an elder has, and where it comes from?

Question 43: How do I determine how much savings an elder has?

Question 44: How do I determine what kind of debt an elder has?

Question 45: Who should pay off an elder's debt?

Question 46: How do I determine if an elder has enough money to pay for food, housing, and medication?

Question 47: How do I determine if an elder's retirement accounts are being withdrawn at the proper rate?

Question 48: Can an elder face penalties if enough money is not withdrawn from retirement funds?

Question 49: How do I determine if an elder has appropriate insurance coverage, and if it can be restructured to reduce expenses?

Question 50: What kind of senior services might be available to help?

Question 51: Who should pay for housekeeping?

Question 52: Who should pay for interior and exterior maintenance of an elder's home?

Question 53: Who should pay for home and appliance repairs?

Question 54: Who should pay for any necessary remodeling to satisfy an elder's living needs?

Question 55: Who should pay for assisted-living services?

Question 56: Who should pay for alert systems?

Question 57: Who should pay for an elder's travel expenses?

Question 58: How do I plan for emergency travel needs?

Question 59: Should an elder consider raising additional cash using a reverse mortgage?

Question 60: What are the pros of a reverse mortgage?

Question 61: What are the cons of a reverse mortgage?

Question 62: What happens to the home after an elder dies if a reverse mortgage is used?

Chapter 7: Managing and Augmenting Your Elder's Funds

Question 63: What types of bank accounts work best for managing an elder's money?

Question 64: What forms do I need to fill out to get access to certain accounts?

Question 65: If an elder is receiving government aid, can I supplement that income with my own money?

Question 66: How much money can I give an elder without affecting government aid?

Question 67: What is the best way to give an elder money?

Question 68: What if my parents need money, but I can't afford to give them any?

Question 69: What if my parents are using guilt to get money out of me?

Chapter 8: Dealing with the Costs of Care

Question 70: How do I know if my parents are telling me the truth about their medical expenses?

Question 71: What do I (or an elder) have to pay for, and what does the government pay?

Question 72: What does Medicare pay?

Question 73: What doesn't Medicare pay?

Question 74: What options does a person have to cover the costs not covered by Medicare?

Question 75: How much does an elder pay for the new Medicare prescription drug plan?

Question 76: What's covered under the new Medicare prescription drug plan?

Question 77: What's not covered under the new Medicare prescription drug plan?

Question 78: What are the different types of Medigap policies?

Question 79: What is Medicare Advantage, and what does it cover?

Question 80: What are an elder's options for covering long-term care?

Question 81: Who qualifies for Medicaid?

Question 82: Is a nursing home legally obligated to care for my parent twenty-four hours a day?

Question 83: Can I pay extra to have someone spend one-on-one time with an elder?

Chapter 9: Basics of Estate Planning

Question 84: What is estate planning?

Question 85: Who needs estate planning?

Question 86: What are the financial goals of estate planning?

Question 87: What are the nonfinancial goals of estate planning?

Question 88: What are the tax goals of estate planning?

Chapter 10: To Have a Will or Not

Question 89: What is a will?

Question 90: What are the requirements for a valid will?

Question 91: What are the typical clauses of a will?

Question 92: What are dispositive clauses of a will?

Question 93: What are appointment clauses of a will?

Question 94: What are concluding clauses of a will?

Question 95: What is a no-contest clause in a will?

Question 96: What are other common optional clauses in a will?

Question 97: Who is a personal representative, and what are his or her duties?

Question 98: How does a person amend or revoke a will?

Question 99: What happens if a person doesn't have a will when he dies?

Question 100: What provisions are made for survivors when no will exists?

Question 101: How is the estate distributed if a person dies intestate?

Question 102: What are the disadvantages of intestacy?

Chapter 11: Dealing with Probate

Question 103: What is probate?

Question 104: What property interests are affected by probate?

Question 105: What are the objectives and processes of probate?

Question 106: What are the advantages of probate?

Question 107: What are the disadvantages of probate?

Question 108: How can an elder avoid probate?

Question 109: What are rights of survivorship?

Question 110: What is joint tenancy?

Question 111: What is a beneficiary?

Question 112: How can a government savings bond be used as a will substitute?

Question 113: How can a POD account be used as a will substitute?

Question 114: What are Totten trusts?

Question 115: What are TOD accounts?

Question 116: What are gifts causa mortis?

Question 117: What are revocable living trusts?

Question 118: What are irrevocable living trusts?

Question 119: How can an elder use provisions in contracts to avoid a will?

Question 120: What are the advantages of a will substitute?

Question 121: What are the disadvantages of a will substitute?

Chapter 12: Dealing with Taxes

Question 122: How does preparing taxes differ once an elder starts to collect Social Security?

Question 123: Can an elder earn money and collect Social Security?

Question 124: What happens to earnings if an elder works before reaching full retirement age according to the rules of Social Security?

Question 125: What is the retirement earnings test (RET)?

Question 126: How much can an elder lose in earnings if she fails the RET?

Question 127: What income must be considered when determining whether an elder must pay taxes on her Social Security benefits?

Question 128: How much tax could an elder have to pay on her Social Security benefits?

Question 129: Does an elder have to pay taxes on pensions?

Question 130: Does an elder have to pay taxes on withdrawals from her retirement savings?

Question 131: How do Roth IRAs differ from traditional IRAs when it comes to taxes?

Question 132: Will an elder have to worry about estimated taxes?

Question 133: What is the federal unified transfer tax system?

Question 134: What is a gift tax?

Question 135: What is an estate tax?

Question 136: What is a generation-skipping tax?

Question 137: What is EGTRRA, and how does it affect the federal unified transfer tax system?

Question 138: What is the marital deduction?

Question 139: What is the charitable deduction?

Question 140: What is the applicable credit (or unified credit)?

Question 141: What is the fair market value of an estate?

Question 142: What date is used for the valuation of property?

Question 143: How does a person report and pay federal estate tax?

Chapter 13: Calculating the Estate Tax

Question 144: What are the key parts of calculating estate tax?

Question 145: What is the difference in calculating estate tax versus income tax?

Question 146: What is the gross estate?

Question 147: Which property is calculated in the gross estate?

Question 148: Is life insurance part of the gross estate?

Question 149: How is joint property calculated in the gross estate?

Question 150: Are survivorship benefits (retirement benefits, pensions, annuities) included in the gross estate?

Question 151: What are lifetime transfers, and how are they included in the gross estate?

Question 152: If a person retains a lifetime interest in property, is that included in the gross estate?

Question 153: What is the three-year inclusionary rule?

Question 154: What can be deducted from the gross estate?

Question 155: How are debts, mortgages, and liens deducted from the gross estate?

Question 156: How does a person calculate funeral expenses to be deducted from the gross estate?

Question 157: What administrative expenses can be deducted from the gross estate?

Question 158: Can a person deduct estate taxes paid to a foreign government?

Question 159: What theft and casualty losses can be deducted from the gross estate?

Question 160: What state estate taxes can be deducted from the gross estate?

Question 161: What is the marital deduction, and how is it calculated?

Question 162: How much in charitable contributions can be deducted from the gross estate?

Question 163: What are adjusted taxable gifts, and how do they affect the calculation of the estate tax?

Question 164: What is the gift taxes payable credit?

Question 165: What is the applicable credit?

Question 166: What is the credit for federal gift taxes?

Question 167: What is the credit for foreign estate taxes?

Question 168: What is the prior transfer credit?

Chapter 14: Estate Tax Planning with Your Elder

Question 169: What are the goals of estate tax planning?

Question 170: How can an elder reduce the gross estate?

Question 171: How can an elder preserve or increase the estate tax deductions and credits?

Question 172: How does an elder manage the marital deduction for estate tax planning purposes?

Question 173: What is the power of appointment trust (marital trust)?

Question 174: What is an estate trust?

Question 175: What is the QTIP trust?

Question 176: What is bypass planning?

Question 177: What strategies can be used to combine marital and bypass trusts?

Question 178: How does an elder use the charitable deduction in estate tax planning?

Question 179: What is the remainder trust in a farm or personal residence?

Question 180: What is a charitable lead trust?

Question 181: What is a charitable remainder trust?

Question 182: What are a charitable remainder annuity trust and a charitable remainder unitrust?

Question 183: What are pooled income funds?

Question 184: What is a qualified funeral trust?

Chapter 15: Rules on Gifts from Your Elders

Question 185: For tax purposes, what is a gift?

Question 186: How do I calculate the fair market value of gifts?

Question 187: What are the filing requirements for gifts?

Question 188: What are special valuations for intrafamily transfers?

Question 189: How is the valuation for purposes of gift taxes determined on lifetime transfers?

Question 190: How is the valuation calculated on retained interest trusts and term interests?

Question 191: What are the effects of buy-sell agreements, options, and restrictions on valuation on the gift tax?

Question 192: What is a lifetime transfer, and when is it complete?

Question 193: How does adding a child's name to property affect the gift tax?

Question 194: What is a defective disclaimer?

Question 195: What transfers of property are exempt from the gift tax?

Question 196: What qualifies as an educational exemption?

Question 197: What qualifies as a medical exemption?

Question 198: How do I calculate total calendar-year gifts?

Question 199: What is the annual exclusion?

Question 200: What are gift tax deductions?

Question 201: What qualifies for the marital deduction of gift taxes?

Question 202: What qualifies for the charitable deduction of gift taxes?

Question 203: What is an inter vivos transfer (lifetime gift)?

Question 204: What is a testamentary transfer?

Question 205: What are the advantages of an inter vivos transfer?

Question 206: What are the disadvantages of an inter vivos transfer?

Question 207: What are the consequences of an outright lifetime gift?

Question 208: What is an outright total-interest charitable gift?

Question 209: What is a charitable bargain sale?

Question 210: What is a charitable stock bailout?

Question 211: What is a charitable gift annuity?

Question 212: What is an outright partial-interest charitable gift?

Question 213: What is an intrafamily loan?

Question 214: What is a custodial gift?

Question 215: What is the Uniform Gifts to Minors Act?

Question 216: What are the elements of a gift in trust?

Chapter 16: Using Trusts to Get Your Elder's Estate in Order

Question 217: What are the goals of a trust?

Question 218: What is a minor's trust?

Question 219: What are qualified tuition plans?

Question 220: What are Coverdell Education Savings Accounts?

Question 221: What is a support trust?

Question 222: What is a revocable trust?

Question 223: What is the best way to use a contingent (standby) trust?

Question 224: What are distributional trusts?

Question 225: What is a pour-over trust?

Question 226: What is a dynasty trust?

Question 227: What is a mandatory income trust?

Question 228: What is a Crummey trust?

Question 229: What is a grantor-retained annuity trust?

Question 230: What is a grantor-retained unitrust?

Question 231: What is a grantor-retained interest (or income) trust?

Question 232: What is a qualified personal residence trust?

Chapter 17: Working with Your Elder to Transfer the Family Business

Question 233: How does an elder transfer the business to a family member?

Question 234: What are buy-sell agreements?

Question 235: What are restrictions upon transfer?

Question 236: What are the gift tax implications?

Question 237: What are the estate tax implications?

Question 238: What are the income tax implications?

Question 239: What are the nontax implications?

Chapter 18: Planning Life Insurance Needs with Your Elder

Question 240: What are the key reasons to use life insurance as an estate-planning tool?

Question 241: What is a joint-life policy?

Question 242: What is a first-to-die policy?

Question 243: What is a second-to-die policy?

Question 244: What are settlement options?

Question 245: What types of ownership can an elder have in a life insurance policy?

Question 246: What is a beneficiary designation?

Question 247: What is group term life insurance?

Question 248: If an elder has only group term life insurance, what are her options?

Question 249: What is split-dollar life insurance?

Question 250: What is key-person life insurance?

INDEX